ABANDONED WASHINGTON, D.C.

EVANESCENT CHRONICLES

CINDY VASKO

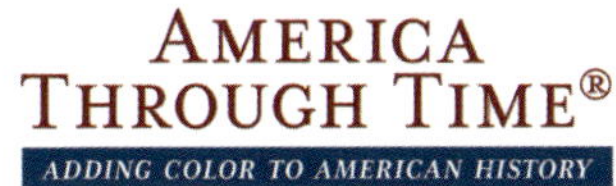

The capability of judging between virtue and corruption is within reach of all. I dedicate this book to the extraordinary hopeful outcomes inherent in the ordinary folks that rock the vote in 2020.

America Through Time is an imprint of Fonthill Media LLC
www.through-time.com
office@through-time.com

Published by Arcadia Publishing by arrangement with Fonthill Media LLC
For all general information, please contact Arcadia Publishing:
Telephone: 843-853-2070
Fax: 843-853-0044
E-mail: sales@arcadiapublishing.com
For customer service and orders:
Toll-Free 1-888-313-2665

www.arcadiapublishing.com

First published 2021

ISBN 978-1-63499-287-9

Typeset in Trade Gothic 10pt on 15pt
Printed and bound in England

CONTENTS

Introduction **5**

1 A Few Bricks Short of a Load **7**

2 Set in Stone **11**

3 The Word Is … **16**

4 The Surround Sound of Art and Nature **21**

5 Down Under **26**

6 The Greenhouse Effect **33**

7 An Artful Spirit **41**

8 Lest We Forget **46**

9 School's Out **51**

10 Don't Drink the Water **60**

11 Old Soldiers Do Not Fade Away **64**

12 Do Not Enter **69**

13 The Words of the Prophets **80**

14 Scraps **84**

15 Silence is Not Golden **87**

About the Author **94**

Bibliography **95**

INTRODUCTION

I moved to Washington, D.C.'s ("D.C.," "District") metropolitan region in the mid-1980s. I was enthusiastic about leaving my birth state, Pennsylvania, for D.C.'s dynamic ambiance—the city on a hill. I love history, political analysis, and exploration, so relocation to D.C. was a good fit for me. Within one week of settlement into my new environment, I was a full-time doctoral student in government and politics at the University of Maryland. Even though I lived in Maryland when I first moved to the D.C. region, and now live in Northern Virginia, my residences were only a few miles from the D.C. border; thus, I considered D.C. as my city, my home. My late husband, an international businessman, and often far from home, allowed ample opportunities for my inner explorer to solo poke in and around D.C. territory.

Frequently, however, D.C. is not an ideal backdrop for urban exploration, because so many forsaken structures vanish in short order. Within D.C.'s hyper-valued real estate constrained footprint, once a building shutters, it is often quickly demolished with something new installed in place. Like so many American municipalities, gentrification patterns are standard features within modern city plans, and D.C. is on track with this development trend. On the other hand, some of D.C.'s abandoned buildings undergo repurposing, especially facilities holding historical status—a good thing in this wasteful society of ours. Some chapters in this book address the new lives given to some historic structures, once abandoned, but now holding a breath of fresh life or one on the horizon.

Additionally, some sites featured in these chapters cut from the usual cloth of abandonments, such as derelict industrial sites, health institutions, and schools. Nevertheless, D.C. is still a bit distinctive from other areas of the country when it comes to addressing real estate statuses due to D.C's often-immediate focus on recouping property via teardowns or reclamations. Despite the good intentions of D.C. city planners and historians concerning its inventory of forlorn structures, I am fearful of a larger insidious trend, a new form of abandonment, gripping my beautiful city, as well as the nation.

Trouble sunders our nation, and especially the power center of our society, my D.C. Deadly coronavirus scorched much of our country, unemployment surged, the economy collapsed, allies look at the U.S. with suspicion and distance, foreign adversaries court some of our political representatives, and weeks of protest and racial disparity left many examining what should be valued and what should be transformed. Our period of national calamity has not encouraged unity; this is a worrisome time in our history. Although this book will be released after our general election in 2020, as I write this, four months shy of the November vote, the United States will make a leadership selection at a time of extraordinary division and chaos. To me, 2020 feels like the longest decade of history. I am exhausted, the District is exhausted, the United States is exhausted, and I think the world is exhausted.

My inner explorer prompted a visit to D.C. at the height of the COVID-19 shelter-in-place orders. I wanted to photograph the silence of Washington, D.C.—the abandonment of the usual rushing environmental din. Never before, at any hour, have I been able to stop in the middle of a busy D.C. intersection to photograph ... anything. I was on D.C.'s Constitution Avenue at high noon and shooting scenes in a stopped car from the middle of a six-lane boulevard. The photographs of silent D.C. are unsettling, unnatural, and so much so that even this photographer, accustomed to shooting urban exploration sites devoid of life, is uncomfortable with such imagery. D.C.'s aura was aberrant and held a firm clutch on anxious silence that I do not want to embrace.

Everything about 2020 is a new experience, and the U.S. appears to be a ship without a captain to steer us out of our danger. The power center of our country is at a stalemate about policy direction. The nation experienced a significant loss of trust in our institutions, a loss in moral guidance, and a great loss of governance. The United States is held hostage within the black hole of abandoned leadership. Will the 2020 national election force abandonment of democracy as well? Will we be able to restore our faith in our institutions, in our leaders, in our foreign relations? As I send this book to the publisher, I do not know the outcome of my concerns with an election still four months away. I remain optimistic that our country's citizens will force a needed change and install political representatives that embrace the reigns of moral leadership and the ideals set forth by the Founding Fathers. When this book is finally released, I hope to live in a world where we can hug our neighbors and not lose our breath with the daily glut of breaking news. While I love all things abandoned, and this is my ninth of thirteen abandoned-themed books, I have no desire to write a book about abandoned democracy.

Our nation requires honesty and courage for a reset and reconnection and not a flight from moral principles. In November 2020, we must continue our journey in the tradition of George Washington, the namesake of my city, and his wish that "the establishment of our new Government seemed to be the last great experiment for promoting human happiness." Mr. Washington's "city on a hill" refers to a community that others venerate. I believed in this community concept when I moved to D.C., and not just for D.C., but for the nation. I think this community essence is still alive, although napping for too long—I hope we rekindle this spirit and not abandon "us."

1

A FEW BRICKS SHORT OF A LOAD

Visiting an abandoned brick factory was my first urban exploration adventure, and these are my initial urbex images that actively launched my preoccupation with this photography genre. My love of urban exploration arrived by accident and occurred in one second. A single word from a research project led to an immediate shift in the motion of my photographic endeavors, and it happened on a Friday evening in July 2012. At this time, I already dedicated three years to photography, especially concert photography. In 2012, I was also the publications manager for a construction law firm. An attorney at the law firm forwarded a request for information about a legal issue concerning a Native American casino in Glendale, Arizona. Trying to keep afloat of my vast workload, I decided to research this issue on my home computer. After taking a short break from several hours of research, I returned to my iMac, and instead of Googling Glendale Arizona casino, I just entered the word Glendale and my page populated with different links, as well as a strip of images about Glendale—but not the casino—the images were of the abandoned Glendale asylum in Maryland. I had a visceral reaction to one photo of the asylum, clicked on it, and advanced to an abandoned photographer's website. I fell into the rabbit hole until 4:00 a.m. as I studied hundreds, maybe thousands of images. I knew at once this was my new photographic path, and within two weeks, my vision was set in motion as I commenced with the urban exploration of the unusual ruins of this brick factory. Touring the forlorn brickworks was a brief matter because my small group had to vacate the premises within minutes, but it ignited an inner fire to carry on with this madness.

Since my relocation to D.C. in the 1980s, I often traveled by this brick facility's strange domes and stocky smokestack resting on a weed-choked concrete slab. The odd cupolas are certainly head turners with a pass of this complex. The beehive-looking structures are furnaces that once fired bricks from clay excavated from the nearby Anacostia River banks. Only the ruins of three kilns remain from the original twelve. In its heyday of operations, bricks from this factory were earmarked for local construction projects, including the New Executive Office Building, and the National Cathedral. The site's roots originated in 1909, but the iconic beehive kilns did not materialize until 1927–1931. The brickworks operated until 1972 when the factory shuttered.

My first urbex adventure was brief—mere minutes—and I had to run from the site. For a second, I thought I was too aged and wise to continue with such foolish drills. After a calming respite post-run, however, I decided to jump into the fray of urban exploration, and this activity has not waned since the brick factory's first. I never returned to this curious industrial plant. I always wanted to revisit it, but thought perhaps I should not tempt fate with a second "run" because my sprinting legs are a bit slower than they were eight years ago, and perchance a minuscule bit of wisdom might intervene within my subconscious and command a cessation such recklessness ... nah! ... crazy is as crazy does, and why not live dangerously while holding on to a few bricks short of a load?

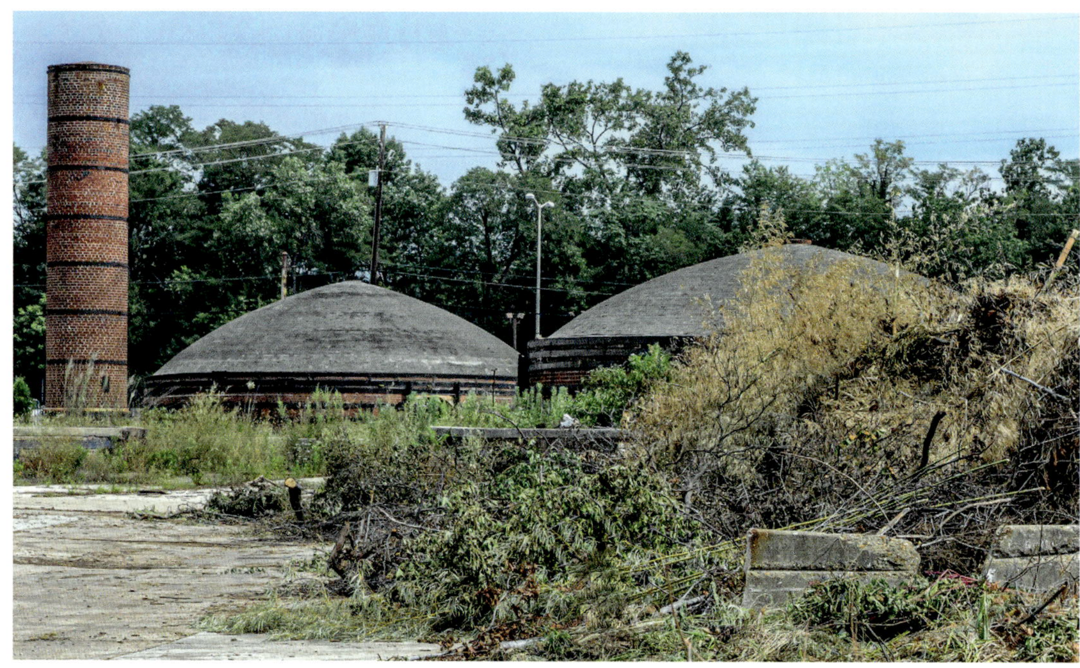

BRICK FACTORY: In the early years of the twentieth century, the Washington, D.C. region held approximately 100 brickyards.

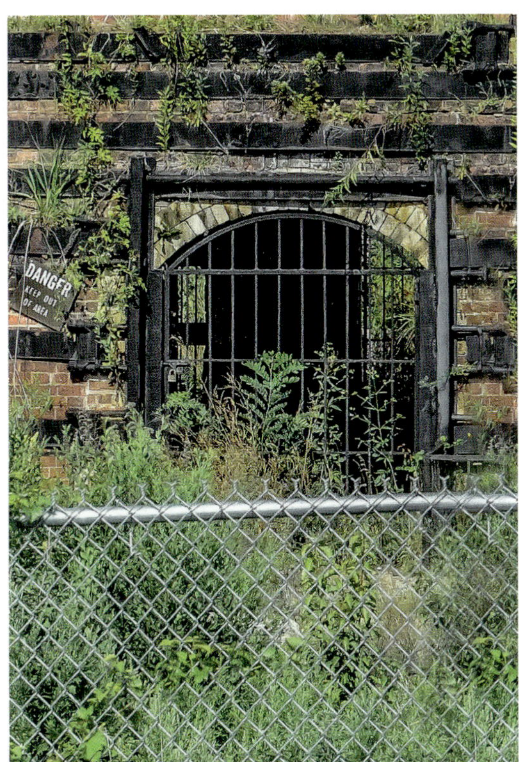

KILN ENTRANCE: The brick factory shuttered in 1972, and in 1978, the complex earned a National Register of Historic Places status.

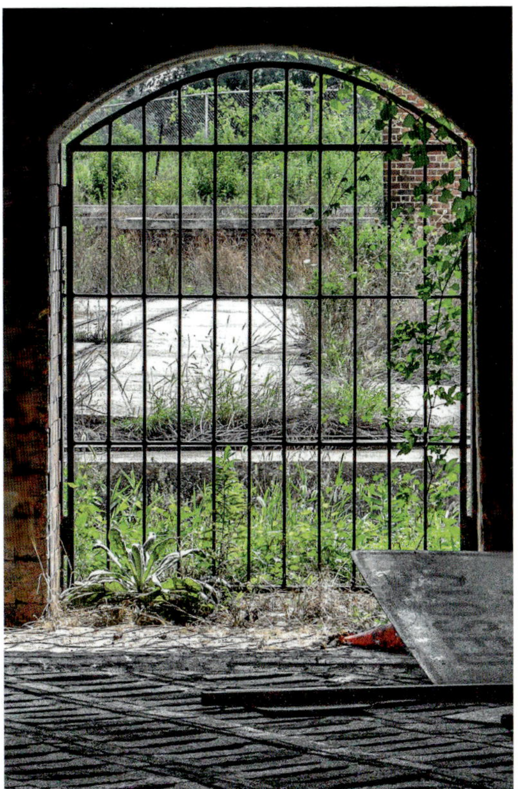

KILN DOORWAY: In 1909, rectangular kilns were built on-site. During 1927-1931, nine circular beehive kilns replaced the rectangular kilns with three additional beehive kilns built after 1931.

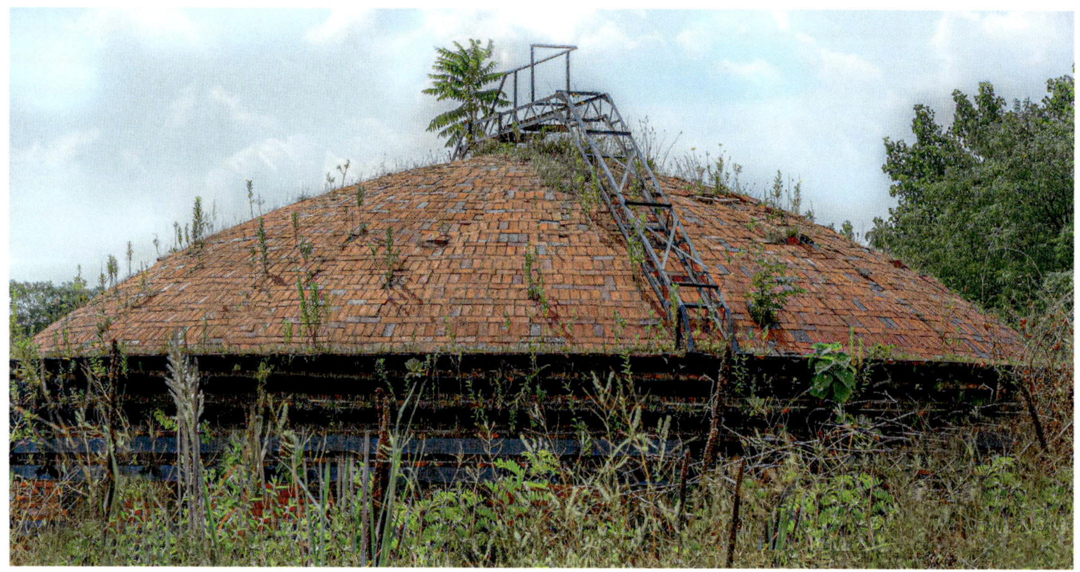

BEEHIVE KILN: Tunnel kiln technology replaced the labor intensive and space limiting operations of beehive kilns.

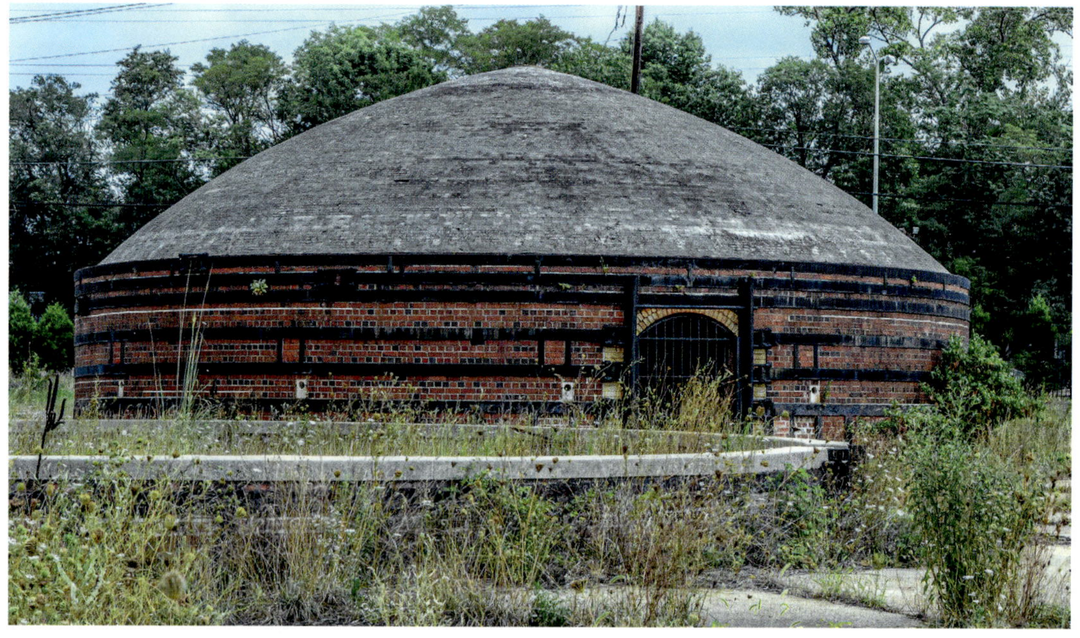

BEEHIVE KILN: Three beehive kilns remain from the original twelve. Bricks fired for four or five days and required two to three days of cooling time.

2

SET IN STONE

The last president to take the solemn oath of office with the backdrop of sandstone Corinthian columns of the U.S. Capitol Building's former East Portico was Dwight D. Eisenhower. Until the Eisenhower administration, the East Portico columns were a presence since Andrew Jackson's inauguration, but for more than six decades, this once revered Capitol facade is no longer a grand symbol of U.S. congressional representation.

In 1824, slabs of sandstone assigned for transformation into majestic columns traveled up the Potomac River to Capitol Hill by way of a manpower-pulled barge, as opposed to mule-powered transport, because these stone slabs were considered sacred pieces and should not be towed by animals. Flash forward to 1958 and the renovation of the East Portico when the facade lost its deferential luster. At this time, the East Portico columns were removed, crated, and stored at Anacostia's Poplar Point Power Plant. The columns remained in their rotting wood crates for decades until a group of women took up the cause to restore the columns' honor and have them stand proudly in the National Arboretum. The old sandstone columns look like ruins from an ancient civilization as they rise from a slope on the vast Arboretum property. Since this is Washington, D.C., though, there is nothing so archaic concerning a city authorized by an Act of Congress in 1790. Still, the hilltop holding these monuments presents proud historical witness and honor.

In addition to the removal of the Capitol Columns, the renovation of the Capitol's East facade, though, was not without controversy. In the late 1950s, the Capitol's fascia was cracking, and at this time, the architect of the Capitol, William Steward, wanted the façade reconstructed in marble. In 1958, the stone frontage, in addition to the column collection, was removed, stone by stone, with each piece cataloged. Even though Georgia White Marble replaced the sandstone, where to store the old stone facade pieces was problematic, and eventually, most stones were unceremoniously dumped in a pile in the woodland of a D.C. park.

For more than six decades, the undisclosed stone pile in the park rests somewhat hidden amidst the vines, weeds, and trees, and although not concealed, and next to a dirt path, the stone piles are often still not manifest to those hiking through the park. Stumbling upon these stones, however, is like a lost civilization scene from an Indiana Jones movie with massive ancient-looking stacks of rock. Some stones hold numerical and alphabetical markings, while others reveal detailed moldings, scrolling, and other design features such as dentil, and egg and dart. All stones are canopied by mature trees, and cloaked in moss with lush crowns of ivy screening them from clear view. Two hundred tons of stone rest on a natural pad of 15,000 square feet. Even though Washington, D.C. is a young city compared to its international counterparts, the stones of the East Portico, nevertheless, illuminate more than 200 years of American saga, and it seems inappropriate not to have such historical markers receive deserved respect instead of languishing in a neglected stone pile in the woods.

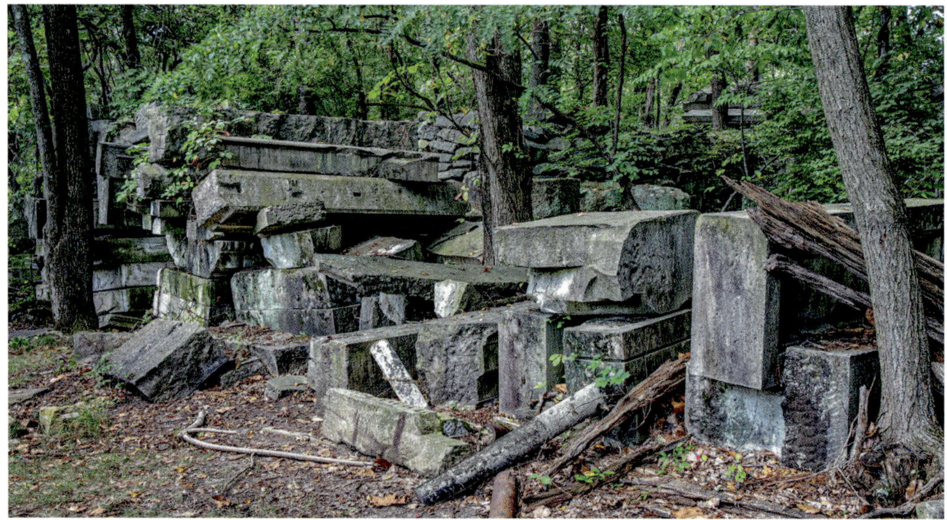

EAST PORTICO CAPITOL STONES: As a result of the 1958 renovation, portions of the original 1828 Capitol East Portico facade rest as a pile of ruins in a wooded park.

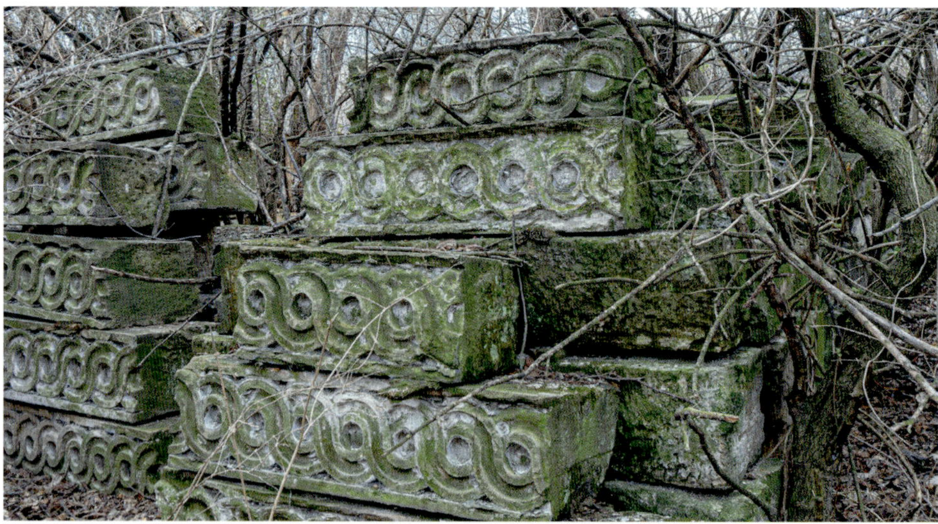

FRIEZE BAND: Sections of the old East Portico's frieze are stacked in a hidden location—far removed from the large depository of stones stacked in a wooded section of a D.C. park.

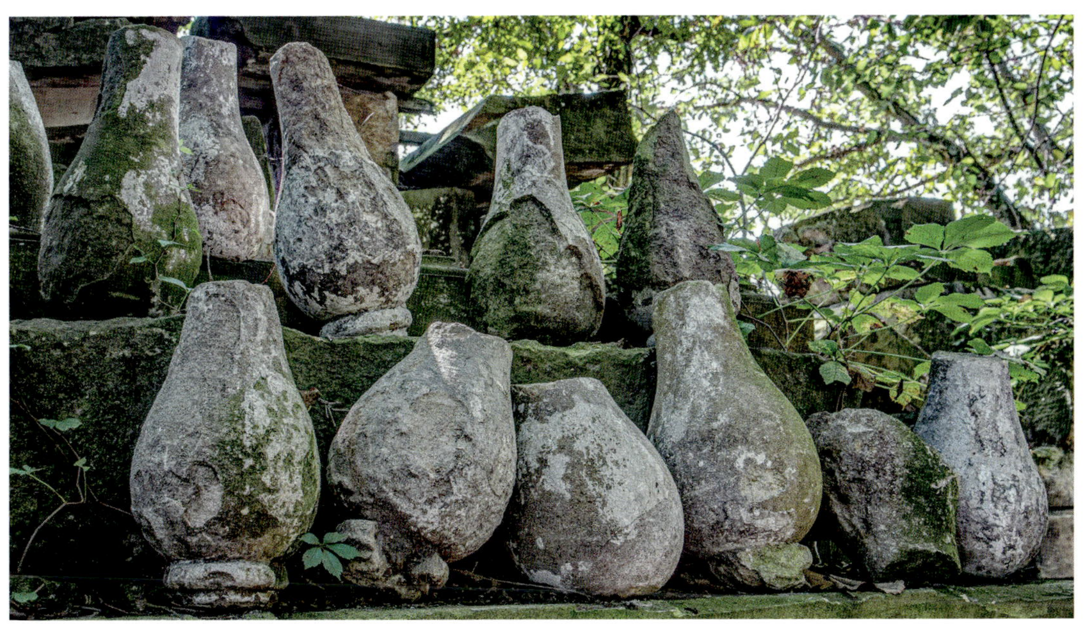

FACADE RUINS: Demolition of the East Portico started in 1958 and continued into early 1959.

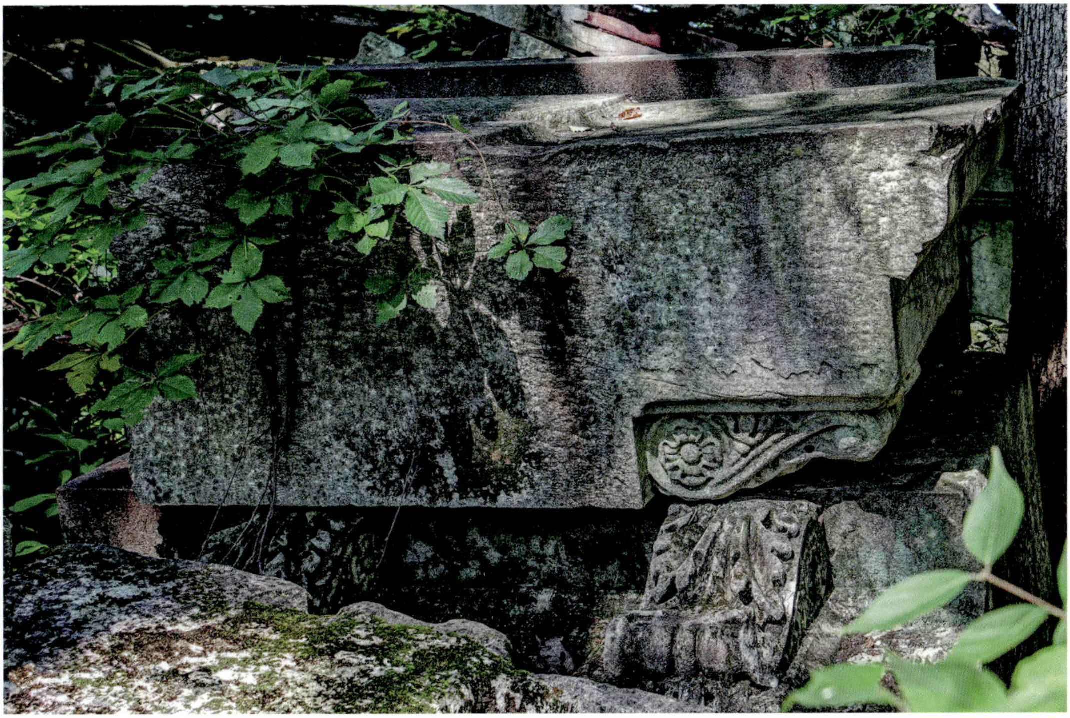

EAST PORTICO STONES: Sandstone, granite, and marble mingle among the 15,000-square-feet, 200-ton stone pile.

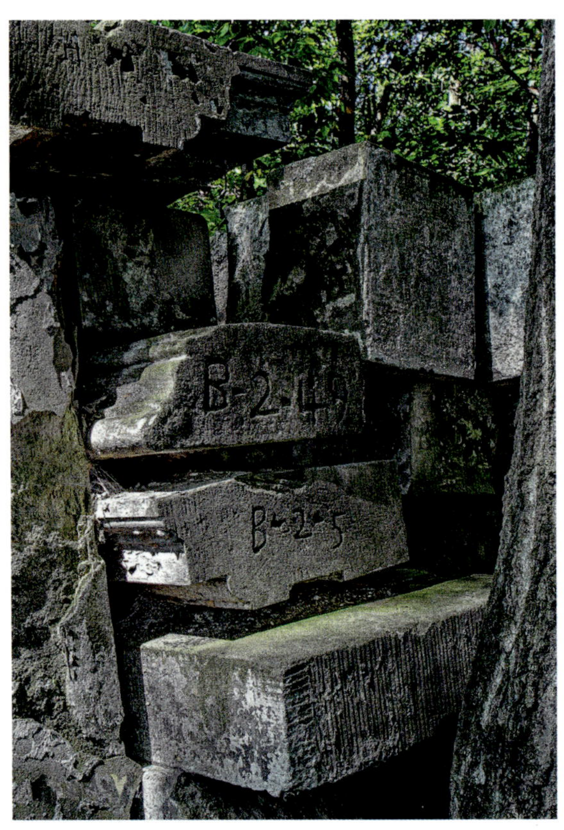

IDENTIFICATION MARKINGS: The stones hold numbered and lettered markings for any consideration of reassembly—like a puzzle.

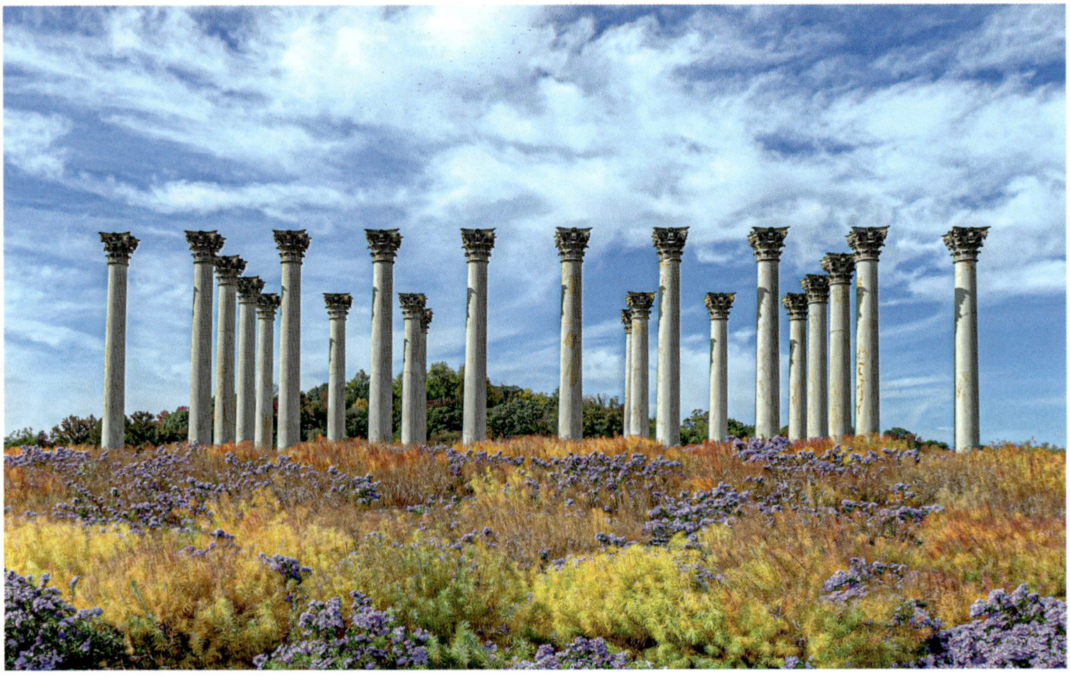

COLUMNS FROM CAPITOL EAST PORTICO: The East Portico Capitol sandstone columns stand tall in the National Arboretum's Ellipse Meadow.

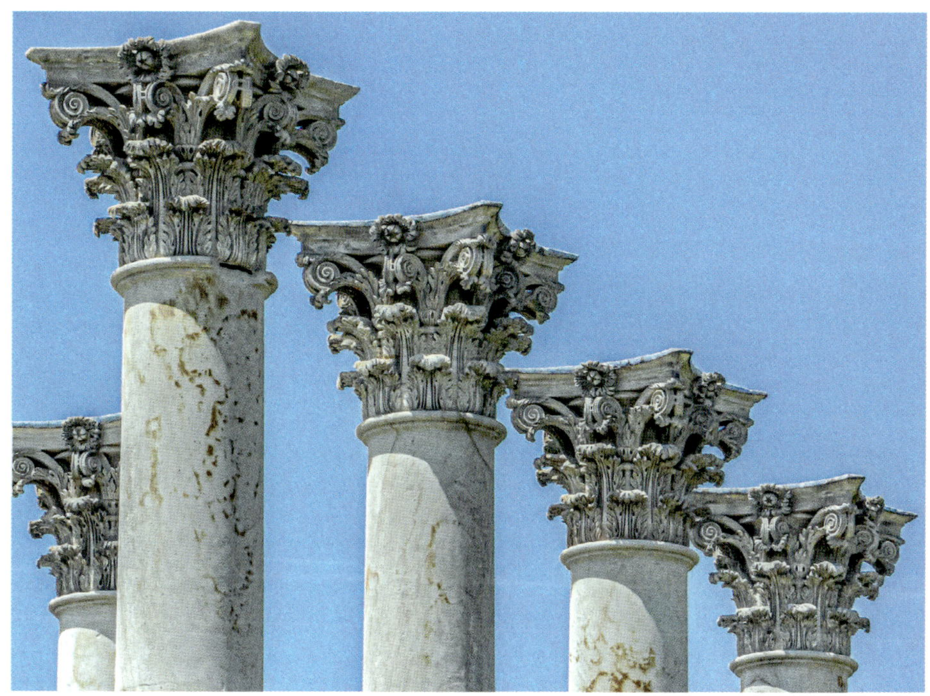

CAPITALS OF CAPITOL COLUMNS: A closeup of the East Portico's Corinthian columns' capitals.

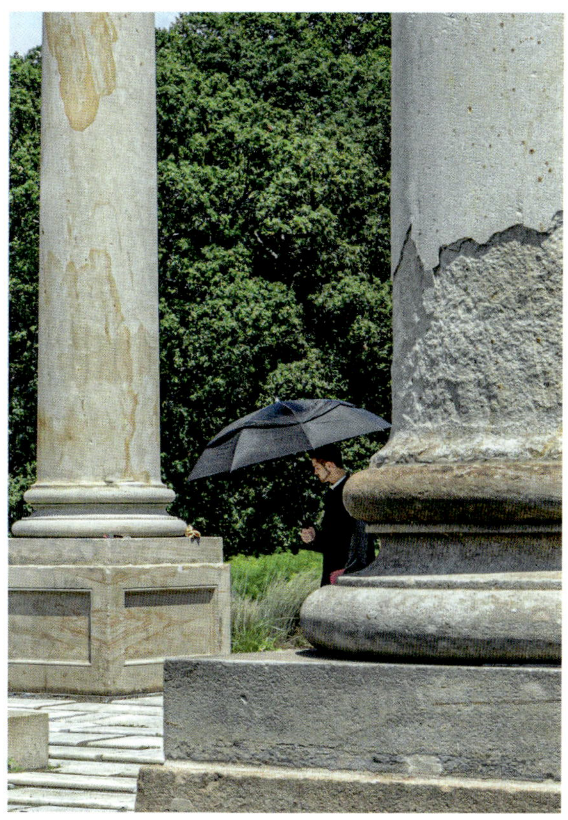

CAPITOL COLUMNS: A presentation of the column size/scale.

3

THE WORD IS ...

When I visited the Benjamin Franklin School ("Franklin") in Northwest D.C., several years ago, the school's exterior appeared structurally sound and well-preserved. I later learned the D.C. government restored Franklin's exterior in the early years of our new century. After stepping foot inside, however, the interior was a bit unkempt, although still clinging to its beautiful architectural details and design—a design that once was the recipient of several design awards for its innovative style.

Franklin is one of the District's oldest buildings and sits only four blocks from the White House. Franklin was the school for the Presidents' children, and the flagship school of D.C.'s eight urban schools erected between 1862 and 1875—all dedicated to a comprehensive plan of universal public education. Established in 1869 as D.C.'s first high school, Franklin's hallowed halls echo weighty history. In 1880, Alexander Graham Bell transmitted his first message by photophone from Franklin's rooftop. Franklin was awarded a National Historic Landmark status in 1996, so its exterior, as well as much of the interior, holds the protection of a historic shield.

Franklin, however, was abandoned for many years but served numerous intentions over the years with a homeless shelter as one of its more recent usages. In the early years of this century, D.C. pondered proposals for the sale of Franklin to real estate developers, but these considerations were met with opposition from community activists, especially with regard to the privatization of public property. In 2008, D.C. closed Franklin's temporary homeless shelter, and the school was again abandoned. A few years later, some members of the activist movement, Occupy Wall Street, broke into Franklin and claimed the school as an encampment for their cause. In short order, the defiant group was removed from the premises, with Franklin returning to a shuttered status.

Franklin, nevertheless, is promised a new life on the horizon. In 2017, philanthropist, Ann Friedman, devoted efforts toward transforming Franklin into an interactive language arts museum, Planet Word. Like so many projects within the District, the Planet Word project has not escaped controversy. Work stoppages as well as criticism for proceeding to renovation before the mandatory historic preservation review process was completed, as well as the alteration of historic architectural features within Franklin's walls, stymied restoration progress. A recent visit to the site a few months ago revealed on-site robust construction and renovation, along with Planet Word signs and banners draped against the old school and on fencing. The Word is: Renewal.

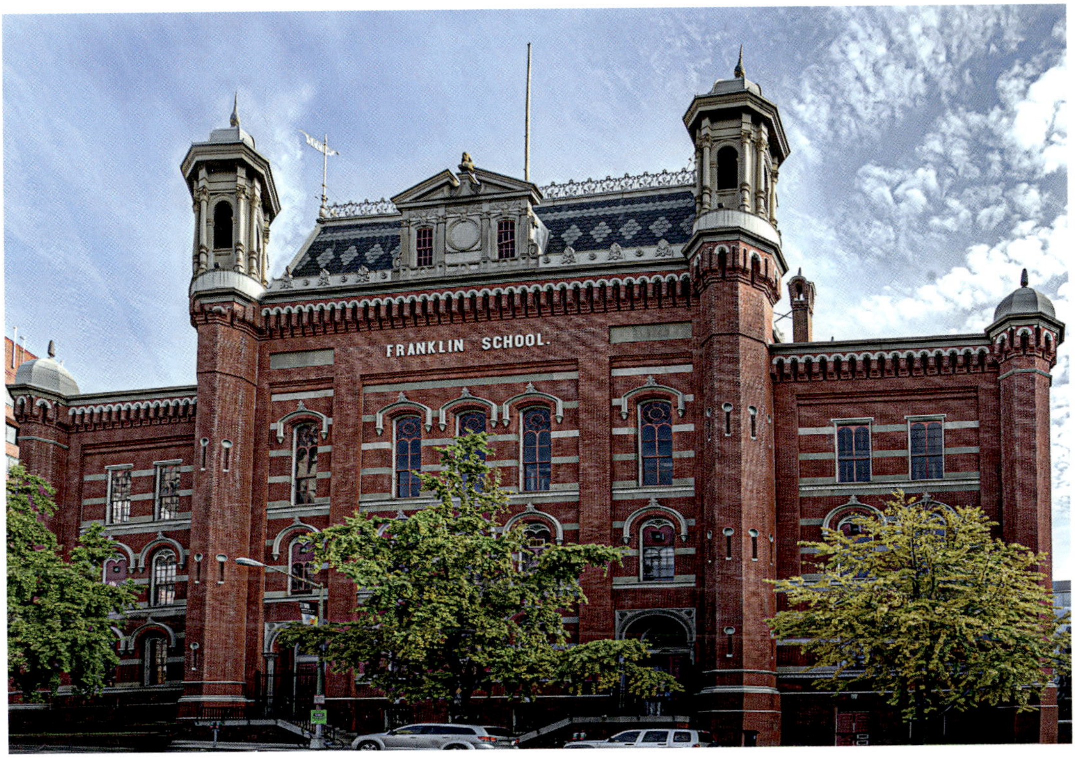

▲ **FRANKLIN SCHOOL:** Franklin's architectural classification is noted as Renaissance Revival.

▼ **CAST IRON WINDOW FEATURE:** Constructed in 1869, Franklin School was the flagship jewel of D.C.'s urban public schools during the late 1800s.

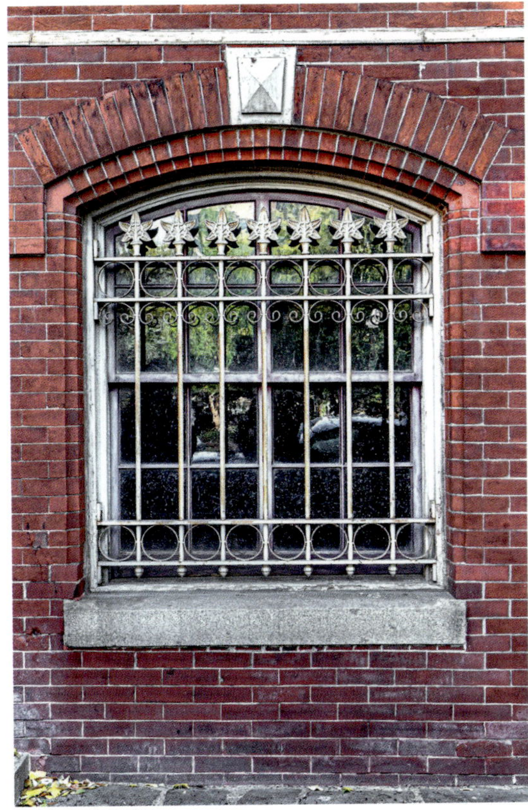

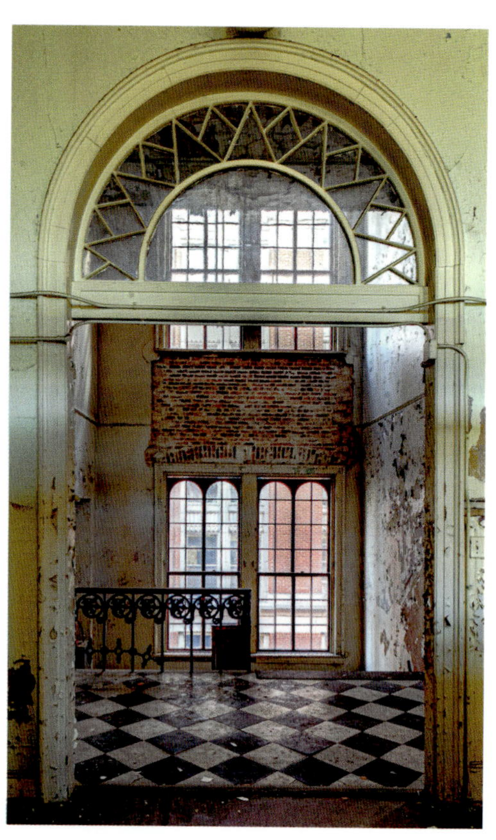

PALLADIAN ARCHITECTURAL FEATURE: Franklin was awarded National Historic Landmark status in 1996.

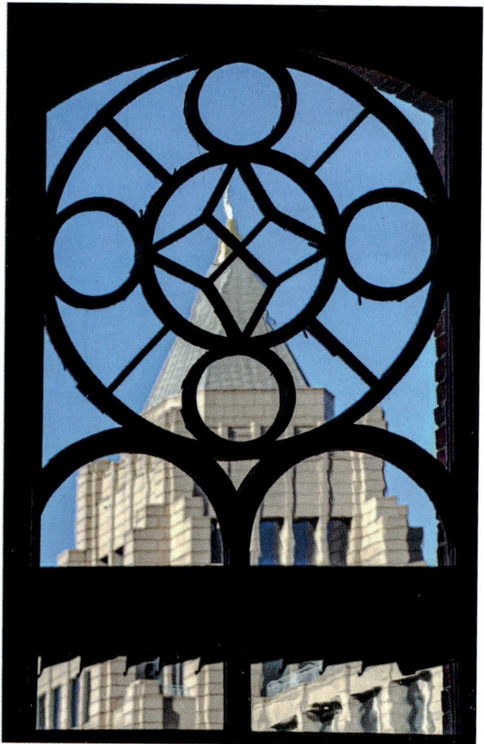

VINTAGE WINDOW-CAST IRON FEATURE AND DISTORTED/WAVY GLASS: Franklin incorporated large windows in its design for the promotion of a bright and pleasant learning atmosphere.

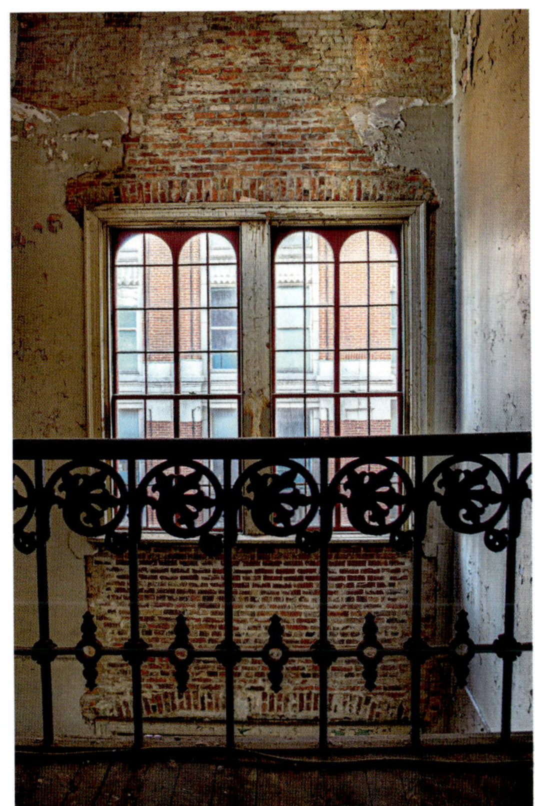

▲ **CAST IRON FEATURE:** In 1880, Alexander Graham Bell administered the first wireless communication on Franklin's roof.

▼ **CAST IRON AND MARBLE CHECKERBOARD STAIRCASE:** Franklin is joined by three building sections and linked by two separate stair and corridor units.

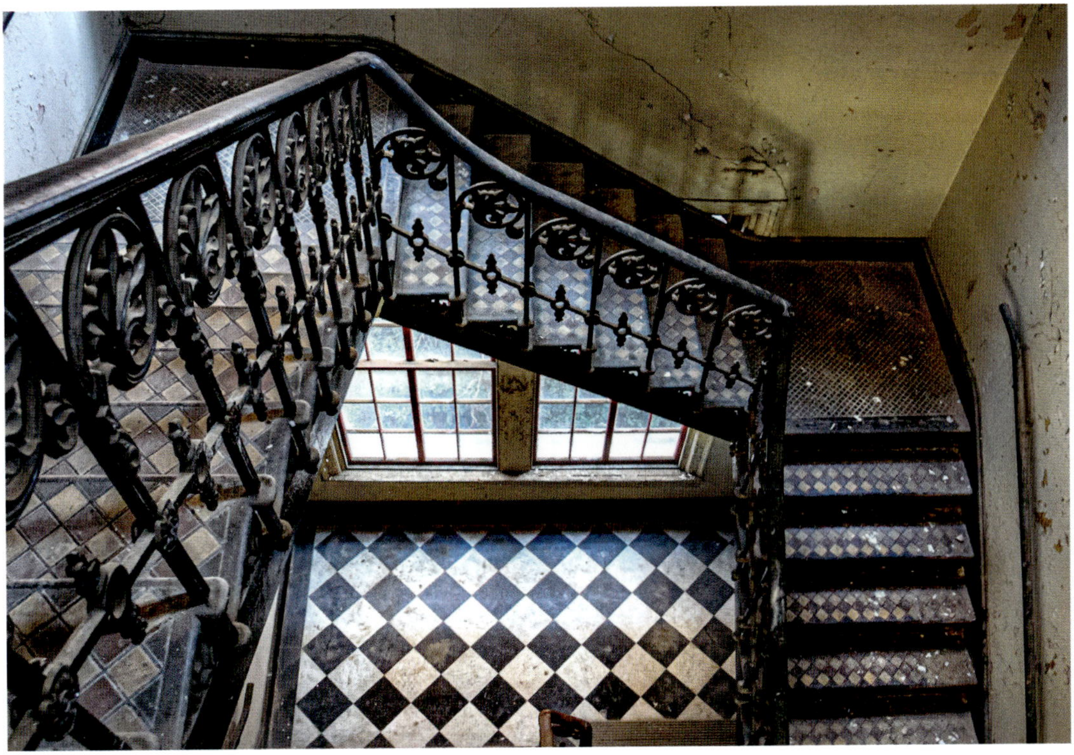

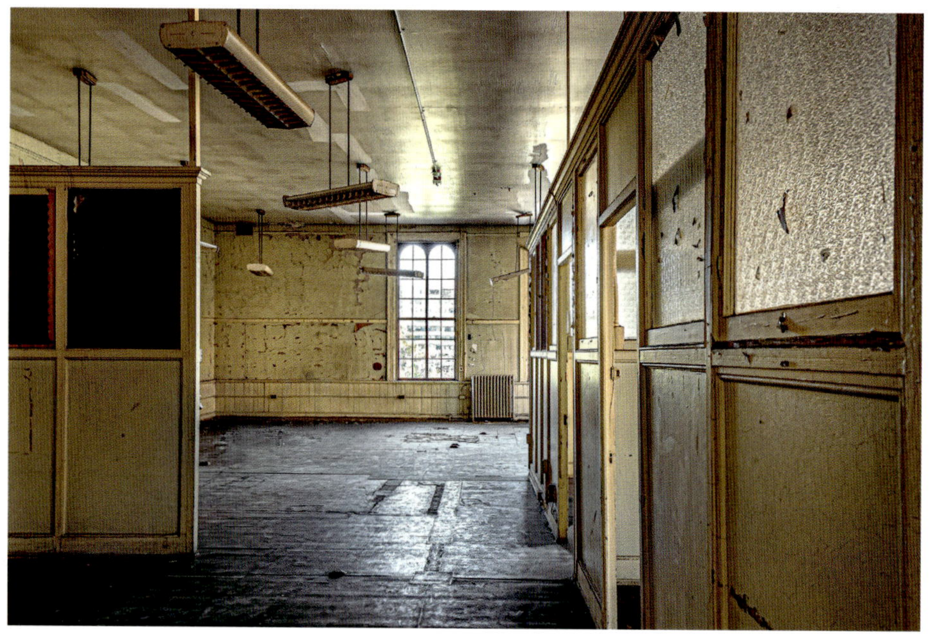

ADMINISTRATIVE OFFICE SECTION: Franklin School was designed to blend with the new federal government buildings, such as the nearby White House and Treasury Building.

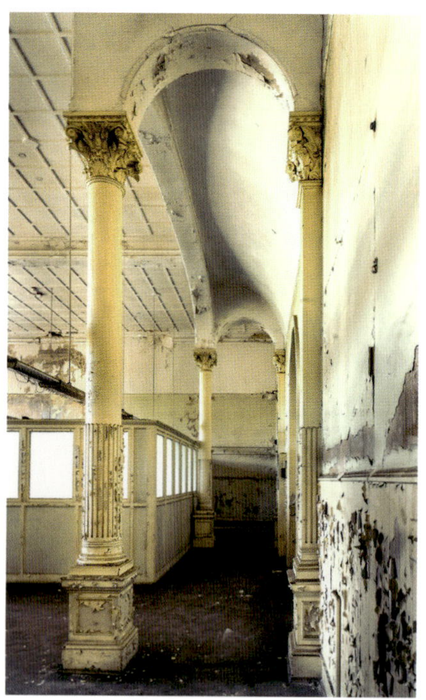

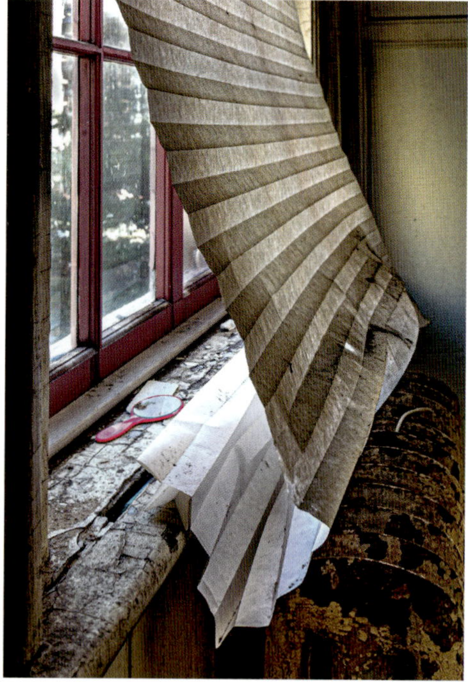

◄ **ADMINISTRATIVE OFFICE SECTION:** Franklin served as a model for D.C.'s developing public-school system and included new concepts of teaching standards, grading, curriculum, and vocational education.

► **REMNANTS OF PAST LIFE:** The construction cost of Franklin School exceeded its estimated cost. Post-Civil War inflation, as well as material and labor shortages, contributed to an escalating budget.

4

THE SURROUND SOUND OF ART AND NATURE

Seeing a beautiful but abandoned outdoor venue with a 360-degree frame of nature grounded in a peaceful wooded setting is bewildering. What better setting for music or events than this locale? At one time, this amphitheatre was one of Washington, D.C.'s best-hidden surprises, even though not secreted when active. In its latter years of activity, most events at this amphitheatre were free, yet the site still did not draw broad interest. Why is such a magnificent setting deserted? Why are we such a wasteful society?

This open-air outdoor theater made its presence known to the public in 1950—during Washington, D.C's 150th birthday. The entertainment venue allowed for upwards of 5,000 attendees to witness varied forms of art and culture. The venue's August 4, 1950, debut event, Faith of Our Fathers, a musical play about the life of George Washington, had President Harry S. Truman seated in the audience.

The golden period for this amphitheatre, however, arrived in the 1960s. Stevie Wonder, Ray Charles, Harry Belafonte, Joan Baez, Nina Simone, Diana Ross and the Supremes, Ella Fitzgerald, along with many additional entertainment headliners, graced the stage with performances. 1967 marked the highpoint year of audience attendance at 200,000. Another good decade, the 1970s, brought forth Bruce Springsteen, Richard Pryor, and John Prine to the grand platform. By the 1980s, though, the venue faced competition from nearby outdoor facilities such as Wolf Trap National Park of the Performing Arts in Virginia, Merriweather Post Pavilion in Maryland, and of course, the District's John F. Kennedy Center of the Performing Arts. The amphitheatre attempted to attract patrons with lower ticket prices but could not compete with the draw at the nearby venues.

By 2013, the outdoor venue held free events, but the scheduled shows were fewer, with only six to seven performances per year from 2013 to 2016. Additionally, structural stage deficiencies were apparent and required reconstruction to meet safety protocols. An engineering assessment determined that the stage assembly was not strong enough to hold the weight of entertainers and equipment, and thus, the venue closed in 2017, and remains closed. I was told the funds are earmarked for repairs of this venue, but COVID stalled such renovation. I have not been able to verify this reconstruction project's actuality, but I hope it is a reality for the near future.

I cannot envision a more beautiful entertainment setting than this facility, surrounded by the drape of nature's hand. It would be such a gift for attendees to see performances in this environment once again, and especially during these turbulent political times—a little escape with music, lush green surroundings, and chirping birds as a bonus, would be good for the soul.

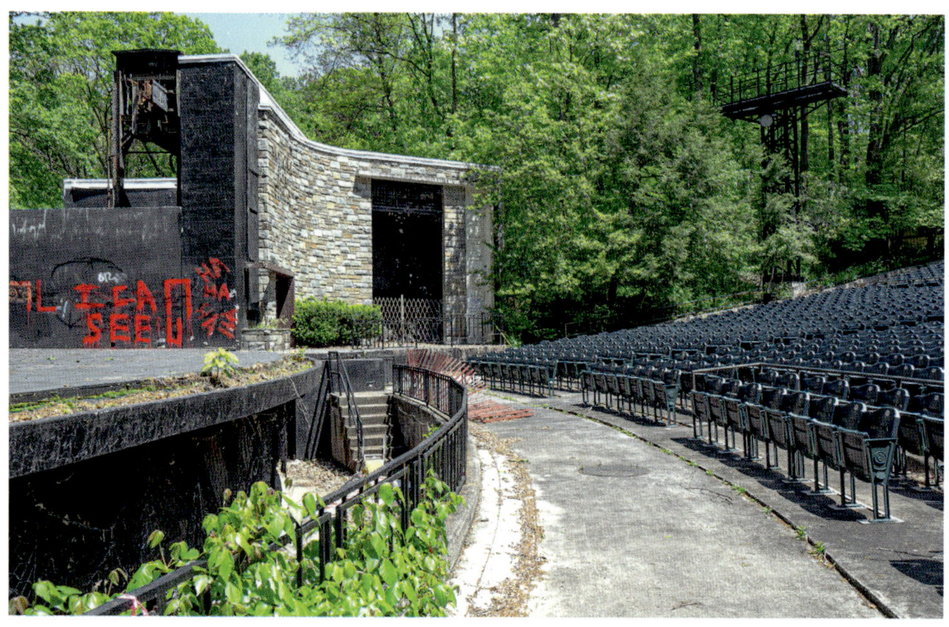

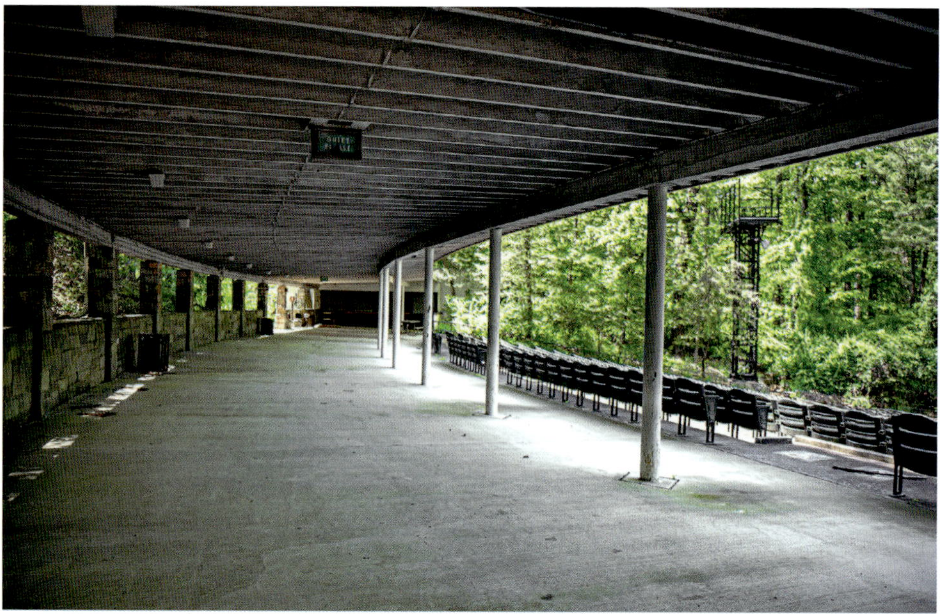

PREVIOUS PAGE:

▲ **AMPHITHEATRE:** The amphitheatre closed for repairs in 2017 following a safety inspection.

▼ **TOP OF SEATING AREA WITH CONCESSION AREAS AT EACH END:** The amphitheatre should realize repairs in 2021-2022 if the venue can acquire the needed funding for stage reconstruction.

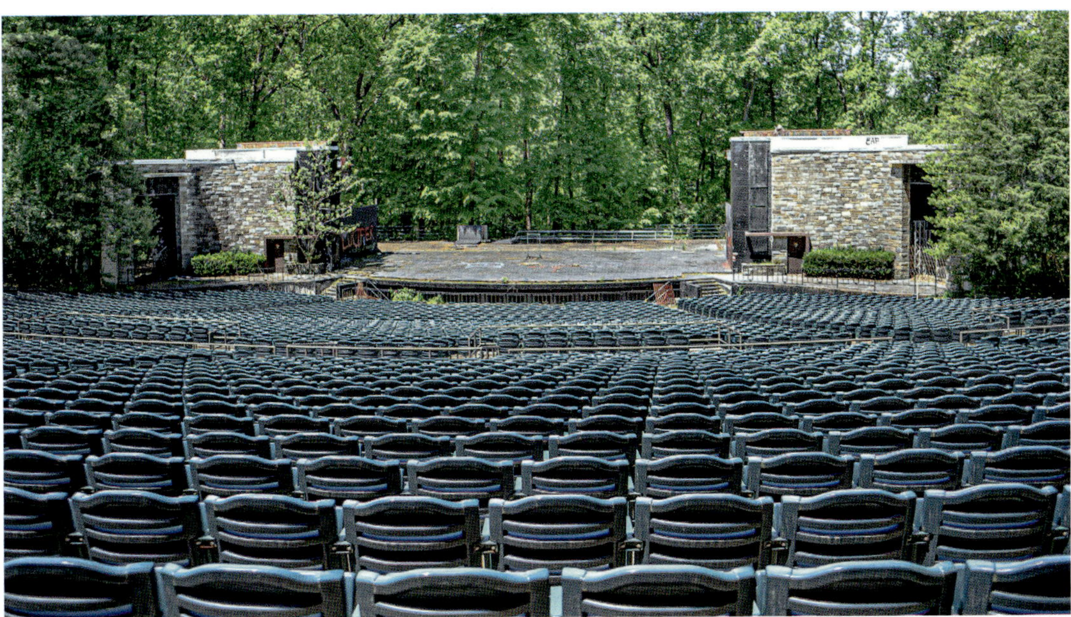

▲ **WIDE VIEW OF SEATING AREA AND STAGE:** The amphitheatre inaugurated in 1950 and in recognition of Washington, D.C.'s 150th anniversary as the nation's capital.

▼ **YES, IT IS QUIET:** The debut event at the venue's opening was "Faith of Our Fathers," a tribute to George Washington, but received mixed reviews.

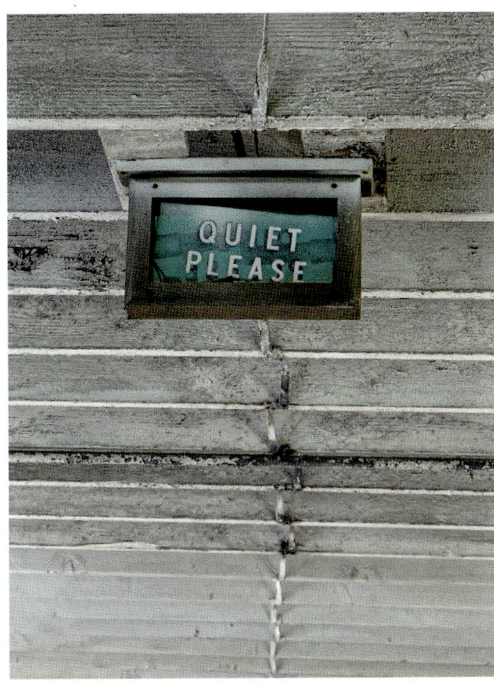

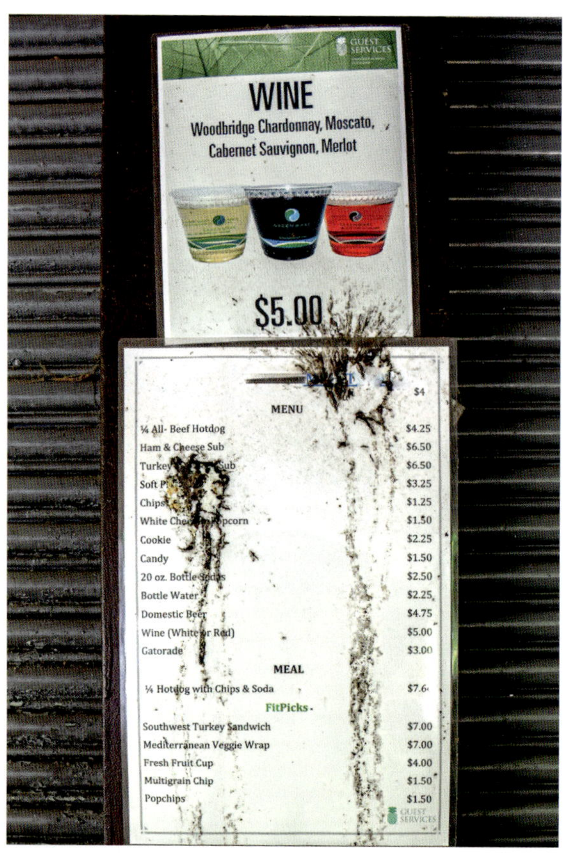

▲ **CONCESSION MENU:**
The location of the venue is seated in a topographical bowl on a hill with maximized natural acoustics.

▼ **STAGE OPERATIONS PANEL:**
In 1965, a curtain and track were added to the stage.

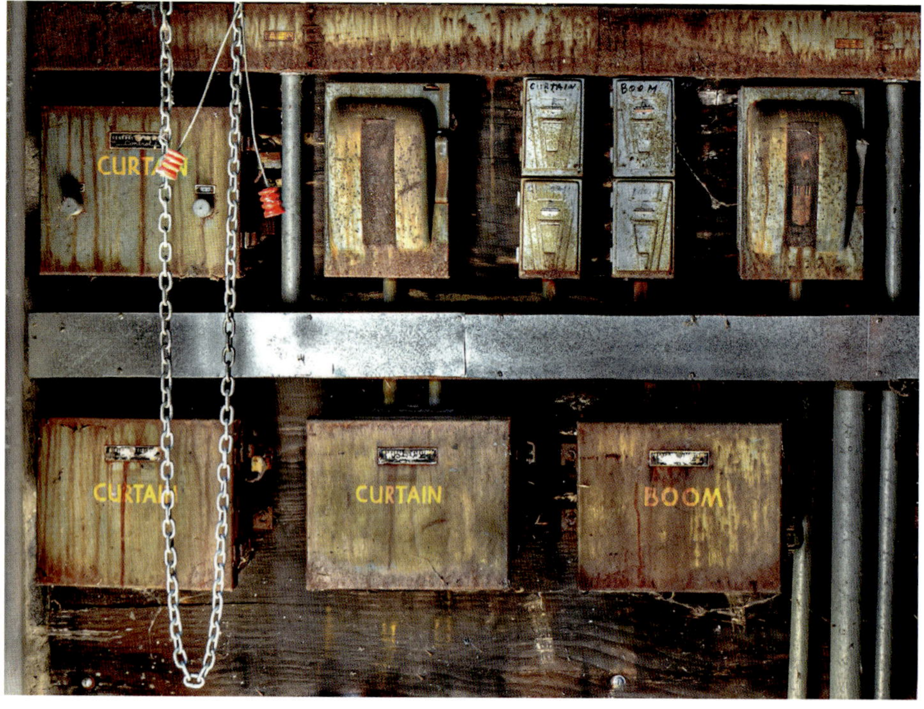

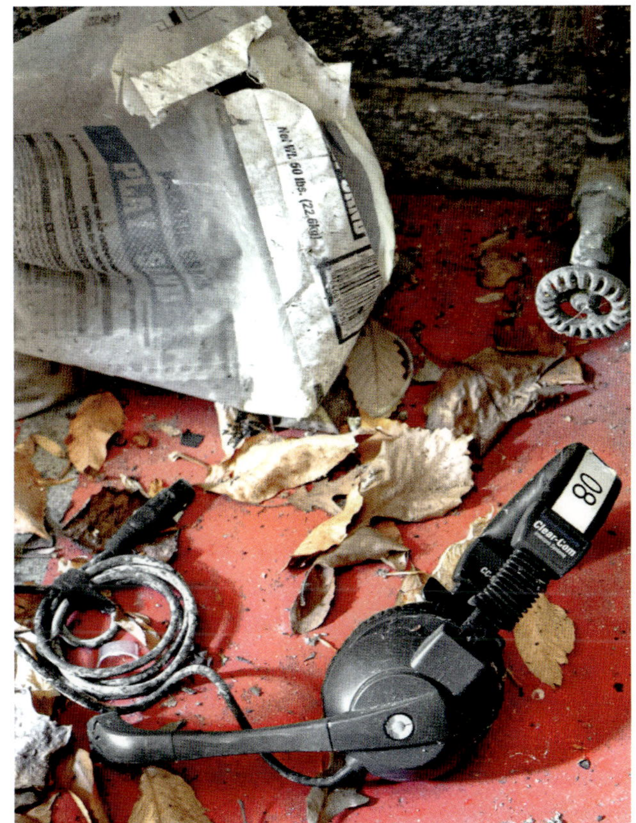

▲ **SOUND EQUIPMENT:** In the early 1990s, the public restrooms were renovated along with electrical upgrades in the backstage area.

▼ **ARE NOT ALLOWED TO HAVE BACKSTAGE PASSES:** In 2003-2004, new seating was installed and incorporated improved drainage within the seating area.

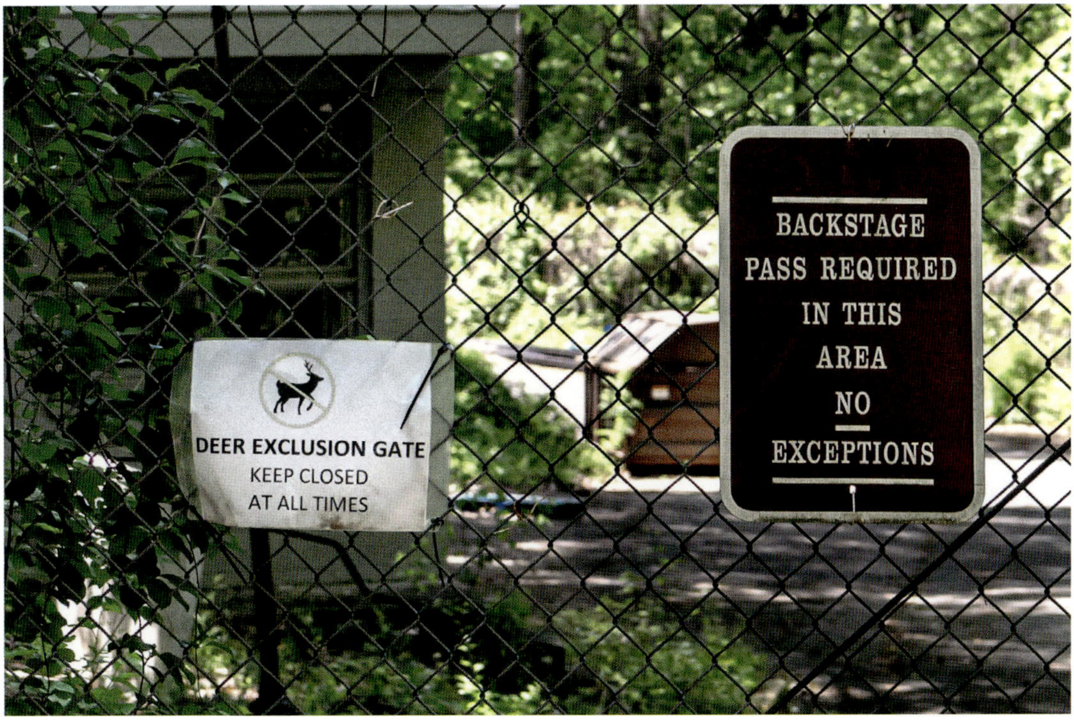

5

DOWN UNDER

Beneath the humming activity of Washington, D.C.'s Dupont Circle neighborhood is a long-deserted streetcar hub, now known as the Dupont Underground. Holding to a series of tunnels and streetcar tracks commanding over 75,000 square feet, the Dupont Underground was once a vital commuter core of D.C.'s transportation plan. This space below the surface of one of D.C.'s busiest communities was abandoned for more than fifty years, vice one short-lived attempt to revitalize a portion of its space.

D.C.'s first electric streetcar debuted in 1890 and captured power from overhead wiring, and later, ground rails. The streetcars provided an alternate means of transportation for the growing D.C. urban center, as horse-drawn transportation slowly faded from the city landscape. Though popular in the early twentieth century, streetcars soon became victims of congestion, delays, and mechanical failures. D.C. was so gridlocked post-World War II that transportation improvements were at the top of the D.C. city planning agenda.

A solution to D.C.'s transportation congestion was to move some of the streetcar lines underground. In concert with the D.C. government in 1949, Capital Transit erected a streetcar station, passenger platforms and tunnels below Dupont Circle. The underground complex held long and vast circuitry and ultimately joined with above-ground streetcar tracks. Even though this design lessened the traffic in Dupont Circle as well as in the contiguous communities, transportation bottleneck issues soon returned and brought forth some added concerns, including a diminution in streetcar participation, labor quarrels, and the ascent of this country's fixation with the automobile. Given all of these competing factors, the streetcar tunnels and platforms shuttered in 1962.

After its closure, the Dupont Underground tunnels served as a fallout shelter, but the vast space was primarily dedicated to the storage of water, food provisions, and equipment. In 1995, the Dupont Down Under project made its appearance as a food court but this endeavor had a short life. The Dupont Down Under project encompassed twelve fast-food vendors but confronted complications from day one of its operations. Beleaguered with poor illumination and unceasing ventilation problems contributing to unpleasant stenches that overwhelmed food merchants and visitors, the Dupont Down Under endeavor buckled in less than one year, and once again, the underground space morphed into a derelict site.

Fifteen years post-closing Dupont Down Under, an alliance of Washington arts representatives came forth as cheerleaders for the preservation of the unique subterranean zone.

The arts visionaries saw the underground space as a foundation for creatives to showcase artistic talent, and their concept became the Dupont Underground. Even though the Dupont Underground arts coalition held some events, the site's future is still uncertain and more so now with the reality of COVID-19. Arts organizations in the Dupont Underground creative alliance struggle for support from grantors, government, and private citizens. Additionally, the arts coalition's lease expired in April 2020, amid the coronavirus pandemic, thus thrusting the future of the space in further jeopardy. The Dupont Underground needs lots of illumination, literally and figuratively, and financial backing to continue with its Down Under arts operations.

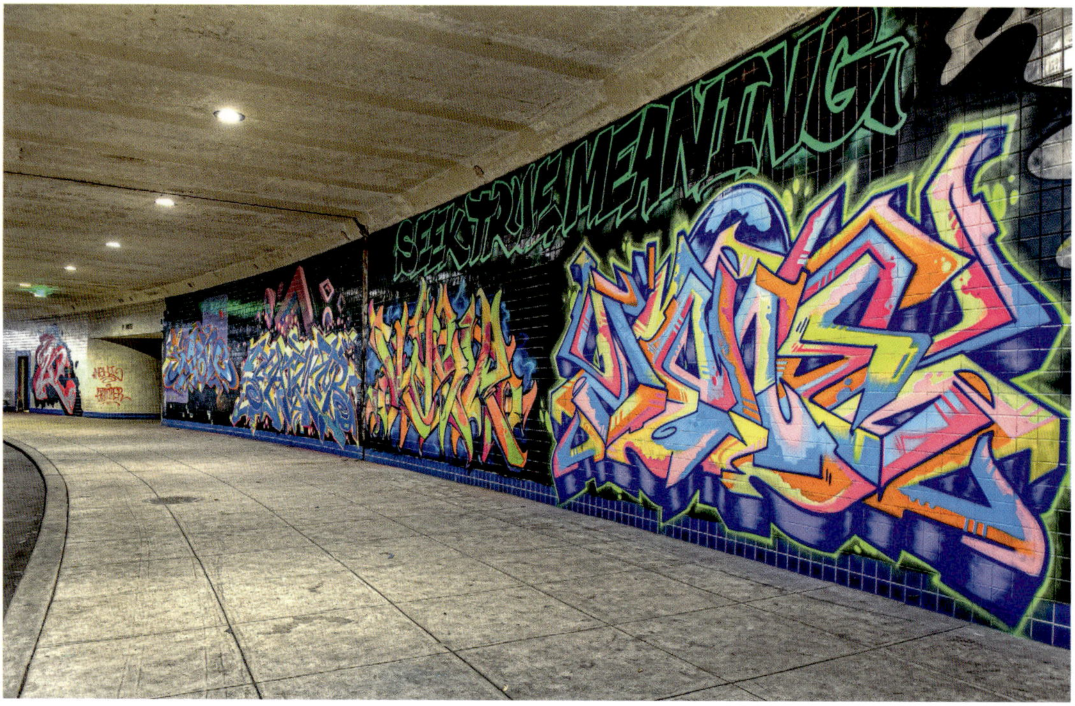

PASSENGER PLATFORM – P STREET ENTRANCE: For nearly a century, streetcars were fixtures in D.C.—originally hauled by horses, and later, electrically operated.

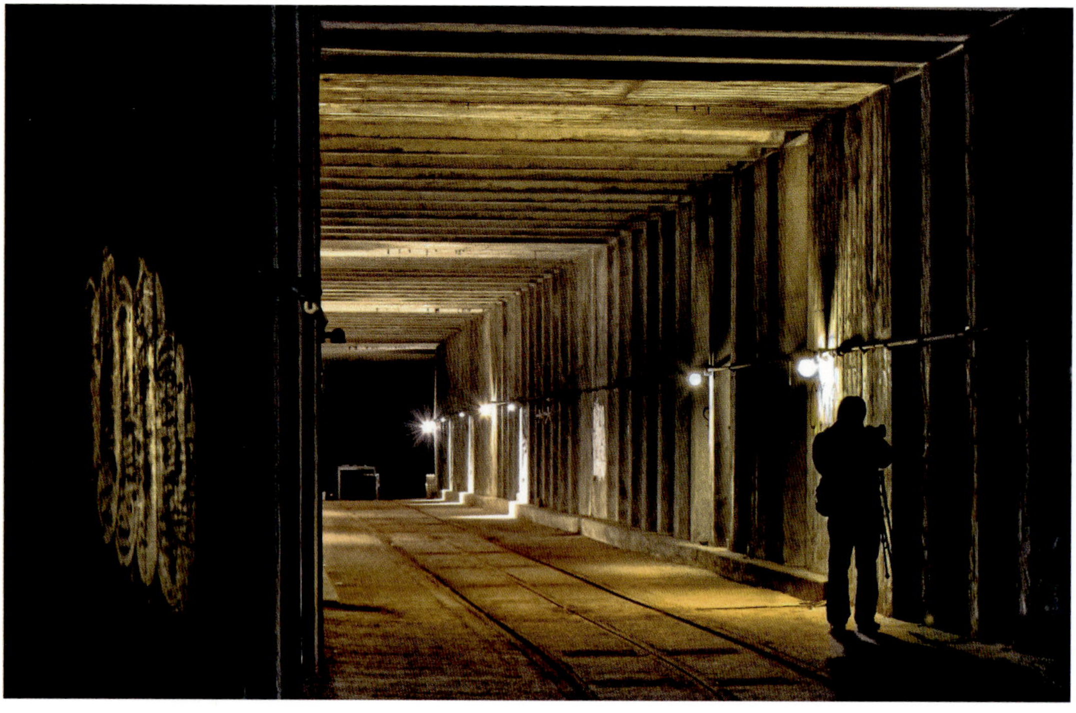

VIEW TO RAIL TUNNEL: In 1949, the Dupont Circle streetcar station was constructed, but closed in 1962, when bus lines expanded, and a new Metro subway system appeared on the planning drawing board.

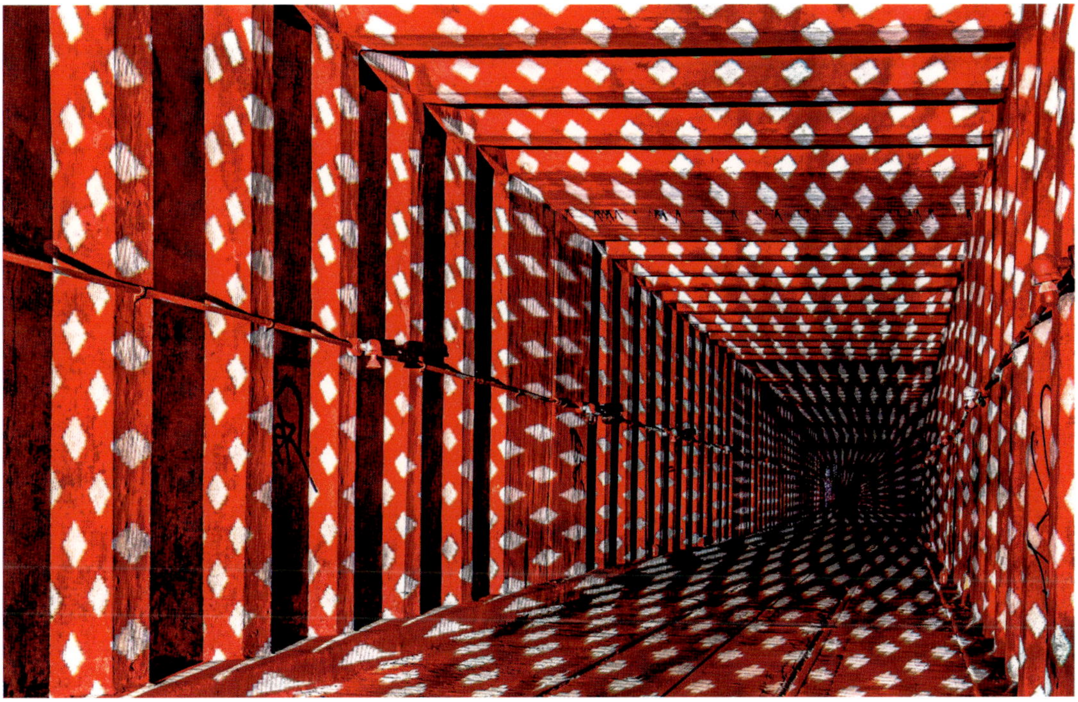

MUSIC AND LIGHT SHOW: The current use of the Dupont Underground is an art space. A music and light show streamed in the rail tunnel.

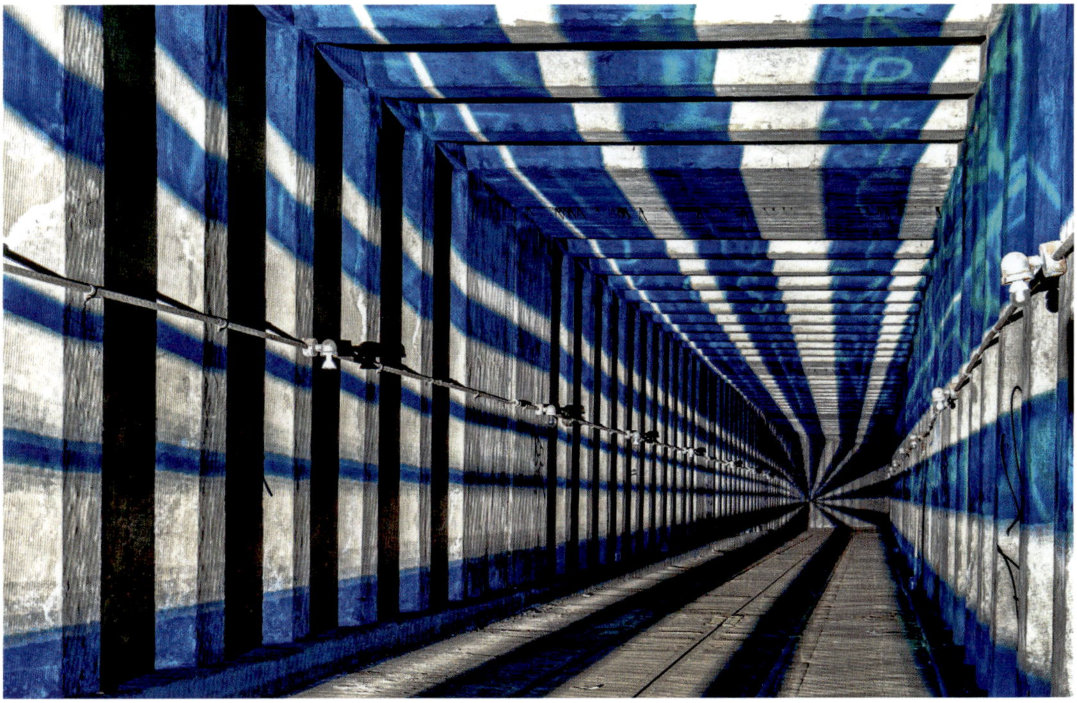

MUSIC AND LIGHT SHOW: After the streetcar station closure, the site was used as a fallout shelter until 1975, when the tunnels were sealed and fully abandoned.

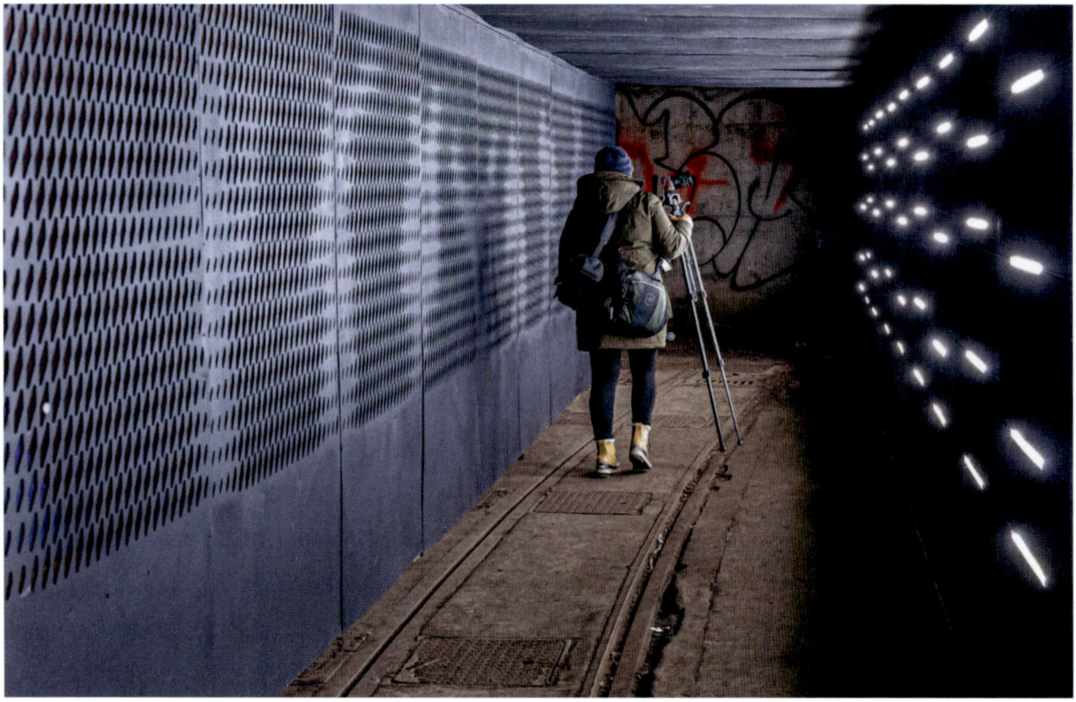

TEMPORARY ART INSTALLATION AND RAIL TRACKS: In 1995, a developer purchased the abandoned space and installed a food court called Dupont Down Under.

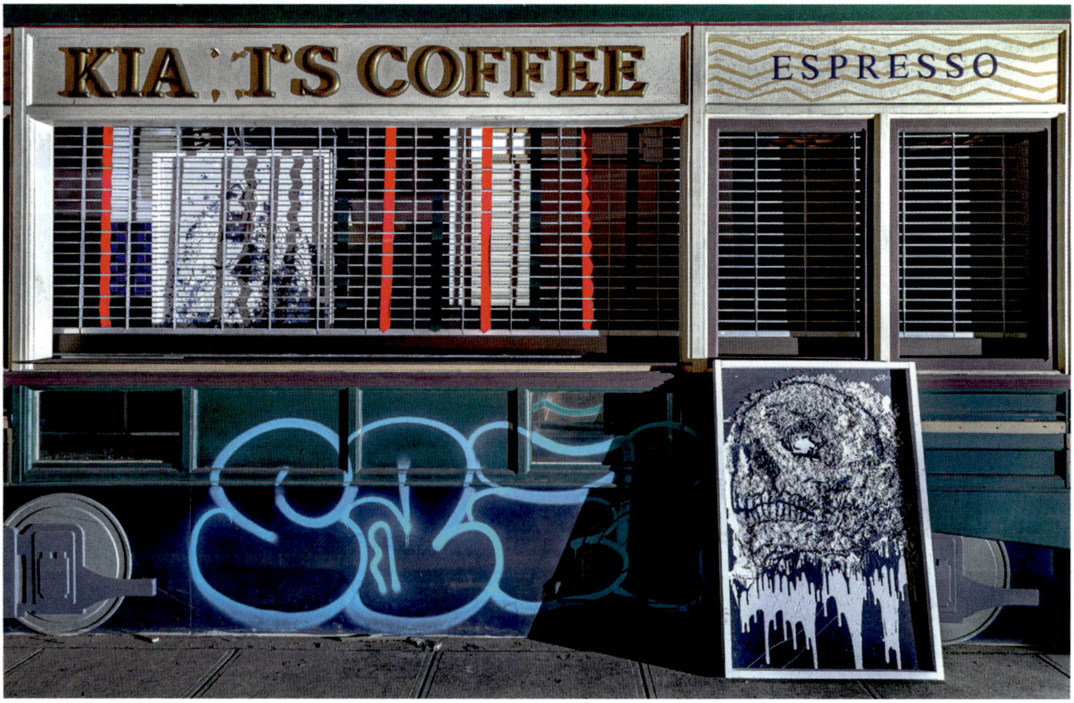

LIGHT-PAINTED ABANDONED FOOD COURT COFFEE VENDOR: Twelve food vendors operated in Dupont Down Under, but the project lasted less than a year.

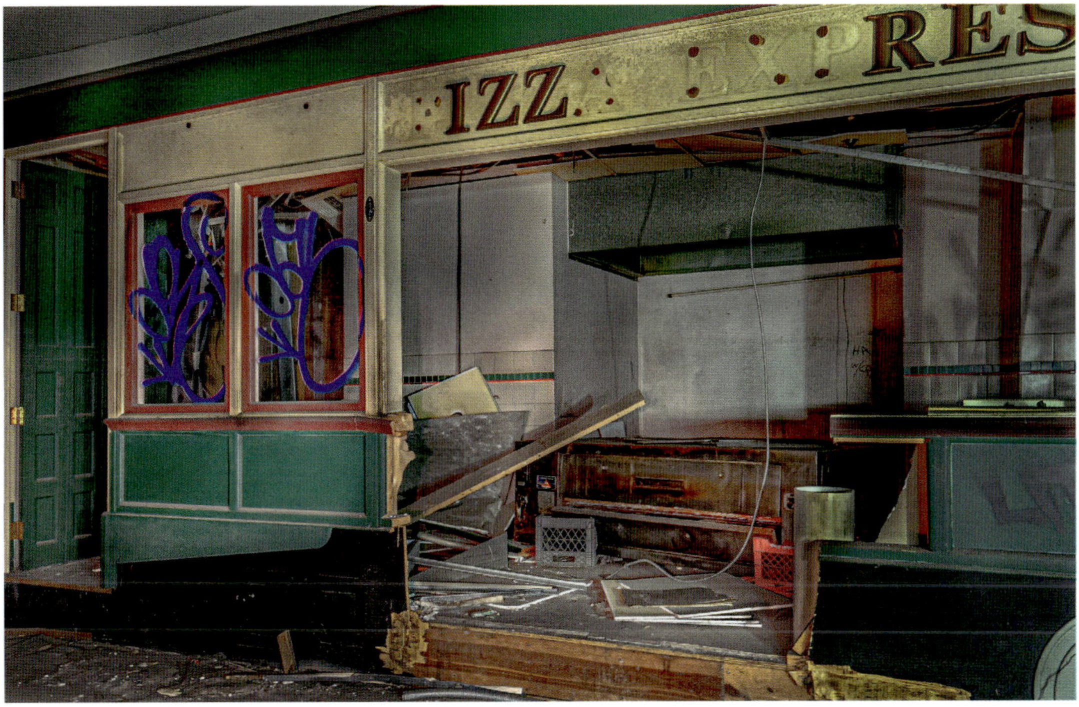

LIGHT-PAINTED ABANDONED FOOD COURT PIZZA VENDOR: In 1996, the underground space was abandoned once again when the food court, Dupont Down Under, failed.

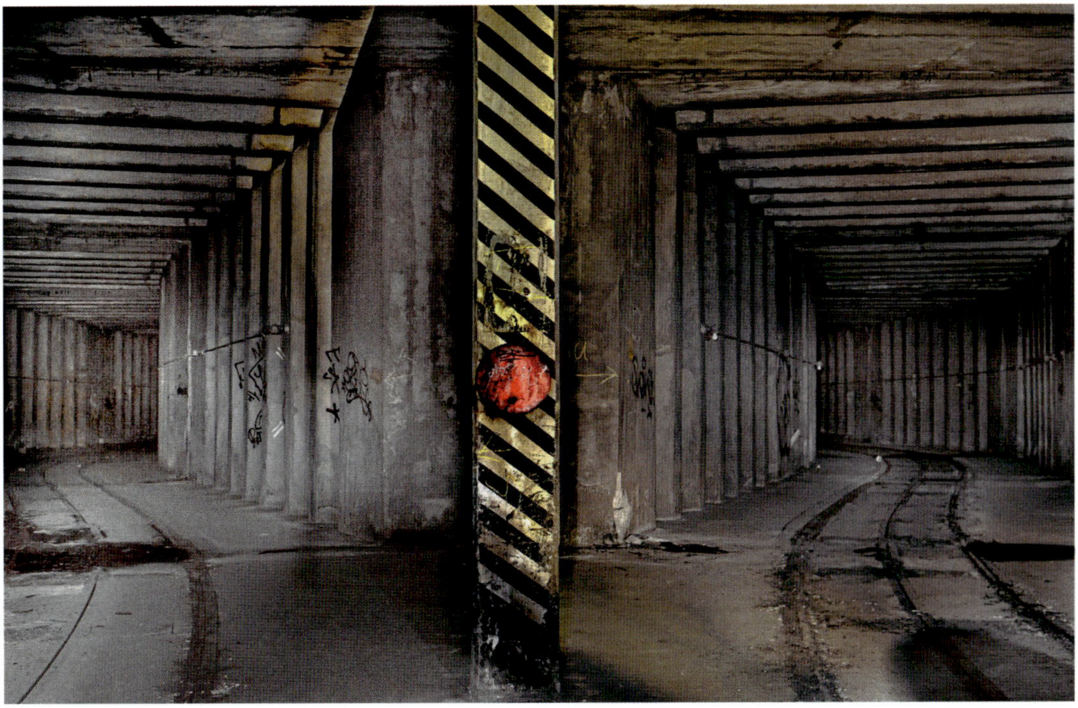

LIGHT-PAINTED TUNNEL TRACK SPLIT - DEEP UNDERGROUND: The first streetcar appeared in D.C. in 1862, via horsepower, and traveled between Georgetown and the Navy Yard.

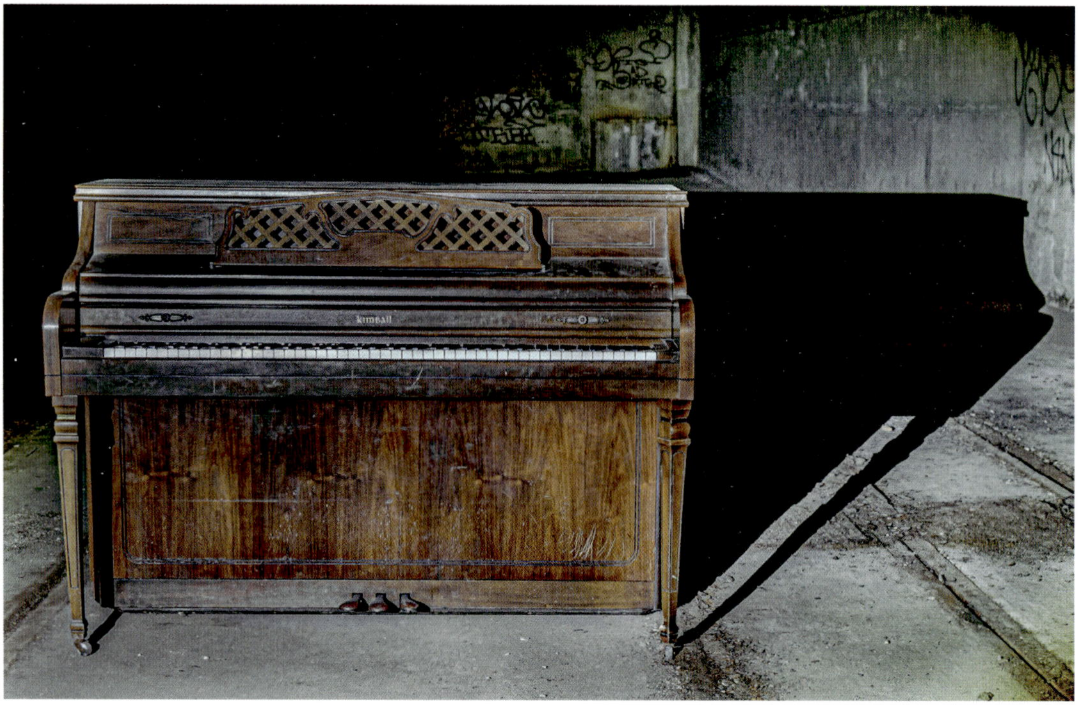

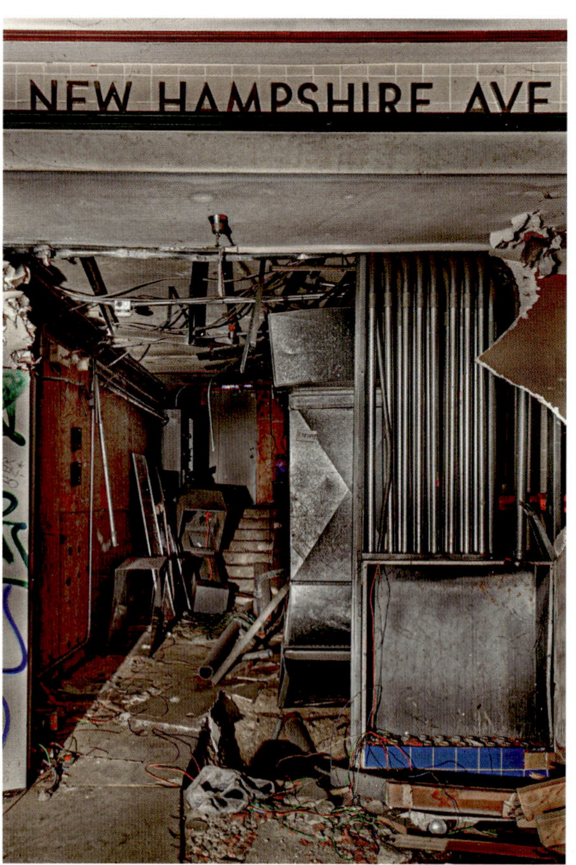

▲ **LIGHT-PAINTED PIANO FOUND ON UNDERGROUND TRACK:** Events on any of the underground's 15,000-square-foot passenger platforms could hold up to 4,000 people.

▼ **LIGHT-PAINTED ABANDONED NEW HAMPSHIRE AVENUE STREETCAR ENTRANCE/EXIT:** In 2016, the 75,000-square-foot space converted into an art space venue. Artists convert the tunnels into art installation spaces and conduct live events that take advantage of the tunnel acoustics.

6

THE GREENHOUSE EFFECT

Capitol Hill overlooks the eastern end of the National Mall. The National Mall is Washington, D.C.'s treasure trove of natural beauty and historical essence. Although the National Mall's appearance has evolved over the years, it was created by the original city plan drawn in 1791 by the French-American Architect, Pierre Charles L'Enfant. L'Enfant's plan had all of the features of a great city—broad public squares and streets, glorious architecture such as the Capitol, White House, museums, and the U.S. Botanic Garden.

The U.S. Botanic Garden, instituted in 1820, is a living museum and one of the oldest botanic gardens in America. The Botanic Garden depends on greenhouses for the propagation of its plants, and since the 1850s, greenhouses obliged the Botanic Gardens. As the Botanic Garden expanded near the Capitol, more greenhouses emerged to house its growing collection. In the 1930s, the Botanic Garden moved from the center of the National Mall to its current location on Maryland Avenue, with production greenhouses situated next to it. By 1956, though, the greenhouses deteriorated, and Congress authorized the demolition of the old greenhouse facilities, but created a new greenhouse site. Plant propagation and storage relocated to a plot of land near the Anacostia River—two miles from the Capitol. This greenhouse complex, under the direction of the Architect of the Capitol, rested on land that was formerly a tidal marsh along the Anacostia River but filled-in to accommodate the new greenhouse and nursery complex supporting the Botanic Garden, as well as the U.S. Capitol.

More than thirty years after its introduction, the greenhouse and nursery complex vacated due to the Washington Metropolitan Area Transit Authority's construction of a nearby subway station. The Transit Authority, in turn, provided the Botanic Garden with a state-of-the-art greenhouse complex on twenty-five acres four miles from the former grounds. The old nursery operations on the Anacostia site consisted of twenty-four greenhouses and operated from 1927 to 1993, but once abandoned, left behind rotting structures, pesticides, and other pollutants. The new production facility assumed operations in 1994. The greenhouse effect of the new facility continues to supply our nation's capital with an endless source of beauty, along with the preservation of L'Enfant's city vision.

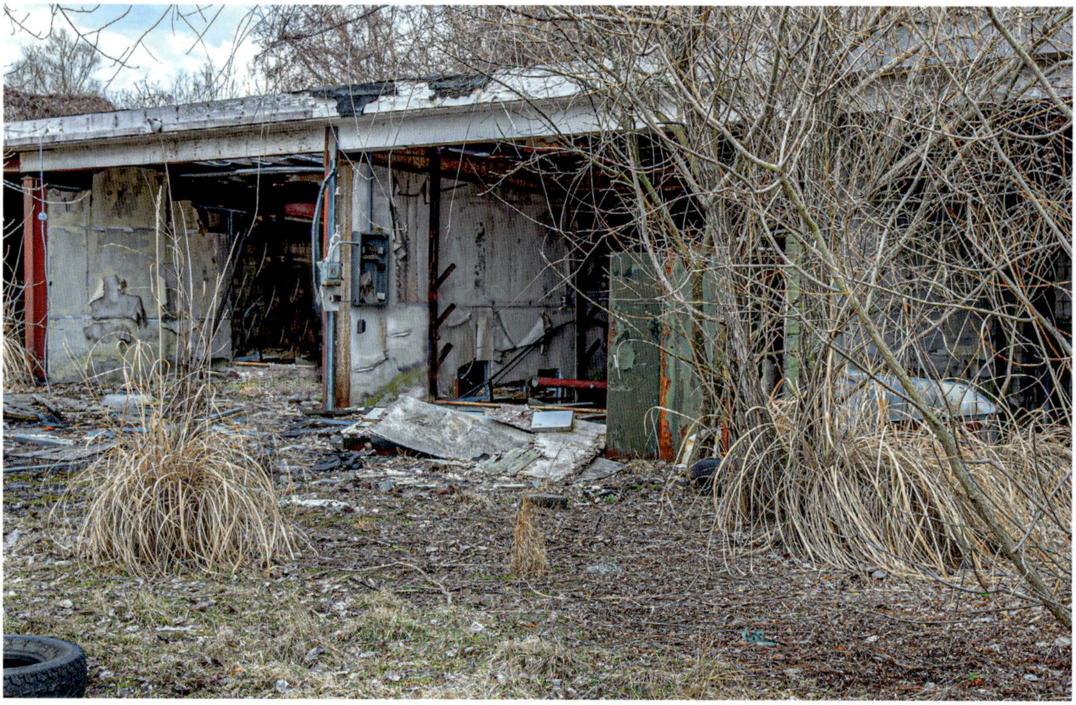

REMAINS OF GREENHOUSE/NURSERY ADMINISTRATION CLUSTER: The 110-acre site, which supported nurseries and greenhouse operations, was active from the mid-1920s to 1993.

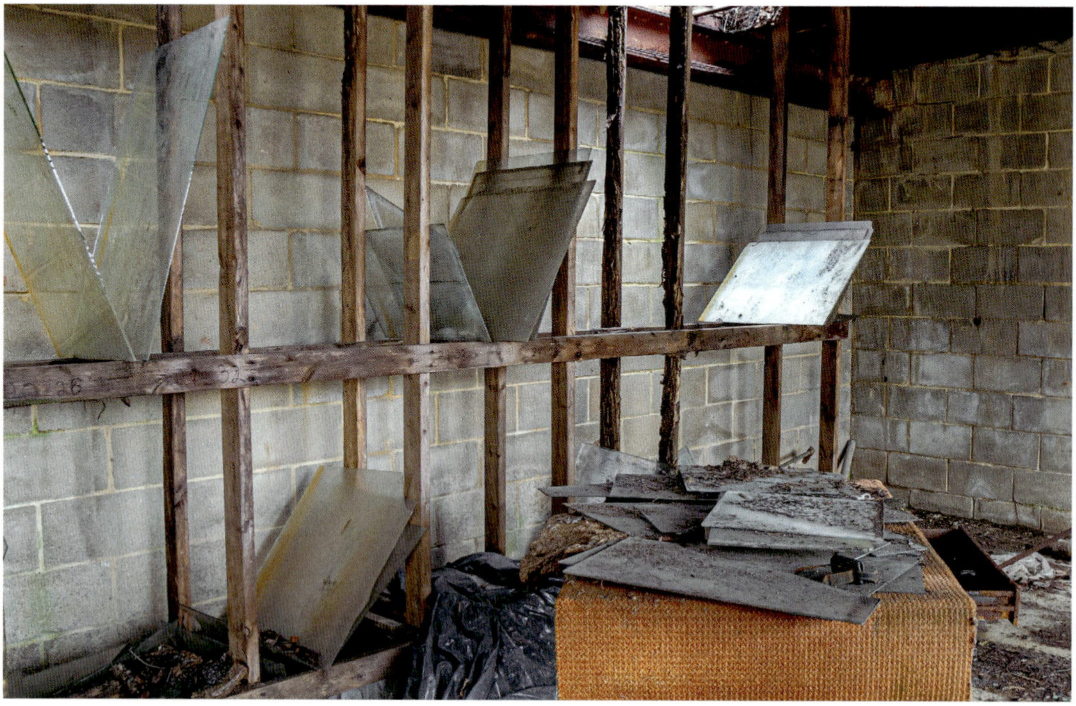

REPLACEMENT GLASS STORAGE ROOM: The greenhouse and nursery site split into two parcels with one devoted to nursery operations and the other managed by the Architect of the Capitol.

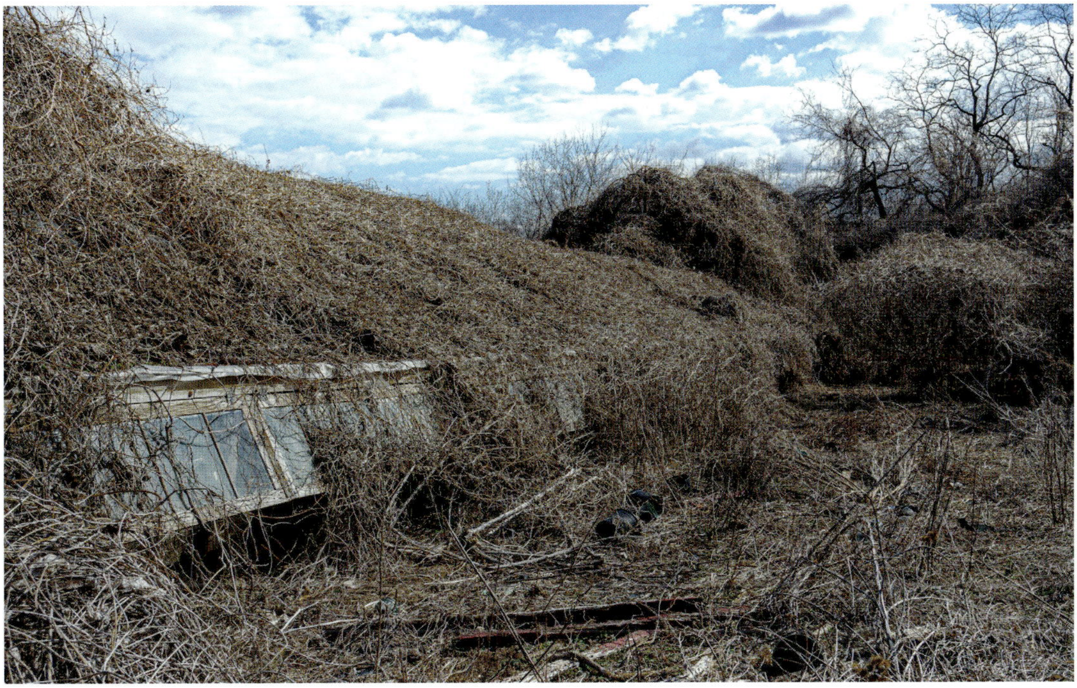

KUDZU VINES JACKET HOTHOUSE BUILDINGS: Pesticides, metals, semi-volatile organic compounds, volatile organic compounds, petroleum hydrocarbons, and polychlorinated biphenyls were found in the site's soil following the shuttering of these operations.

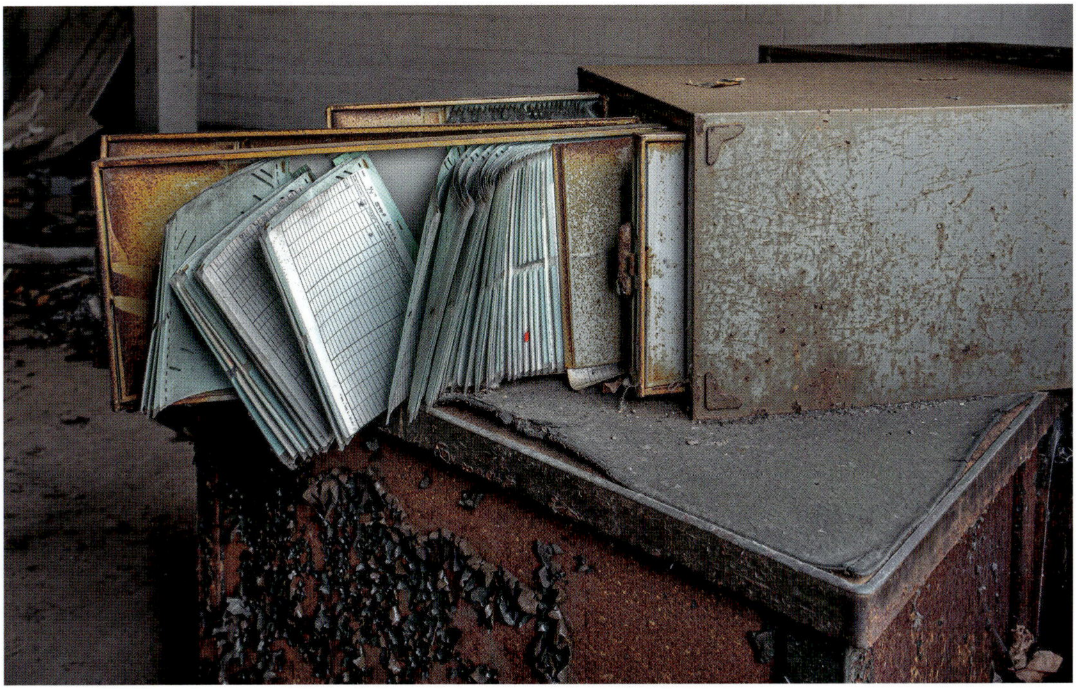

OFFICE FILES: In 1796, George Washington believed a Botanic Garden should be installed in the nation's capital as a living plant museum to highlight the planet's diverse and fragile ecosystems.

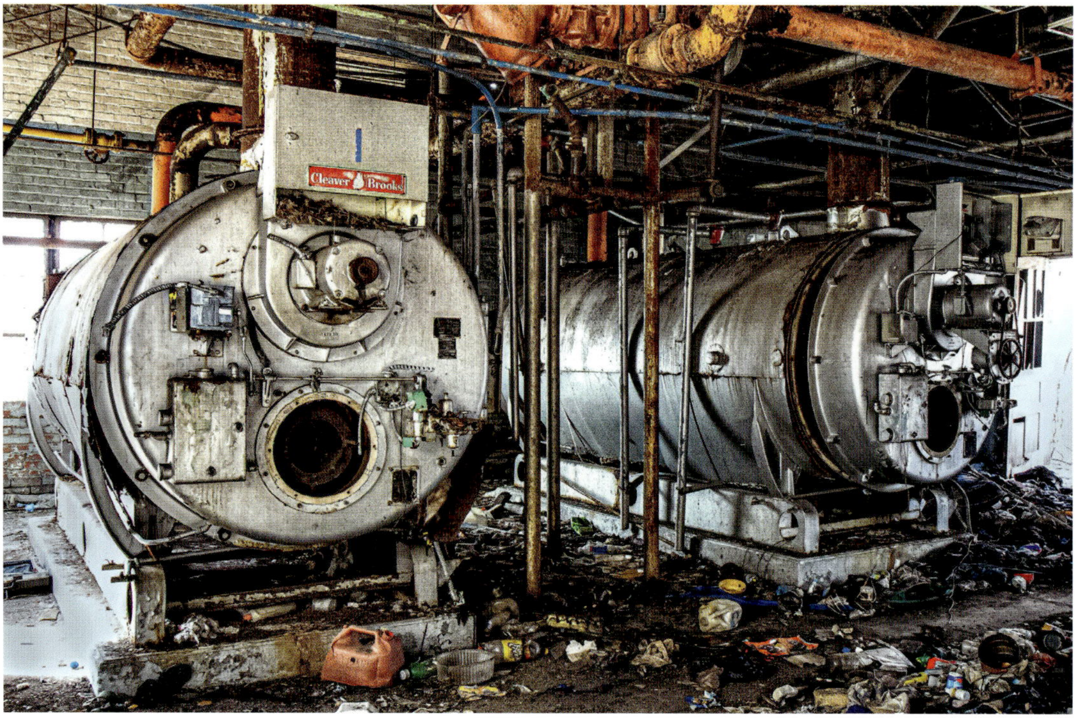

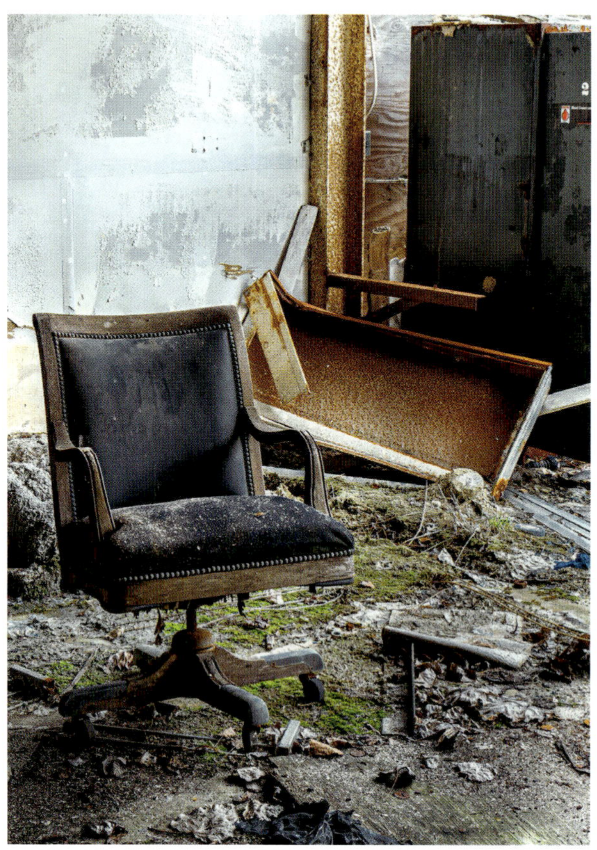

▲ **CHEMICAL VATS:** The derelict nursery and greenhouse site sits on a filled tidal marsh along the Anacostia River—filled between 1882-1927.

▼ **OFFICE FURNITURE:** The government nurseries and greenhouses support the U.S. Botanic Gardens and its draw of more than 75,000 annual visitors.

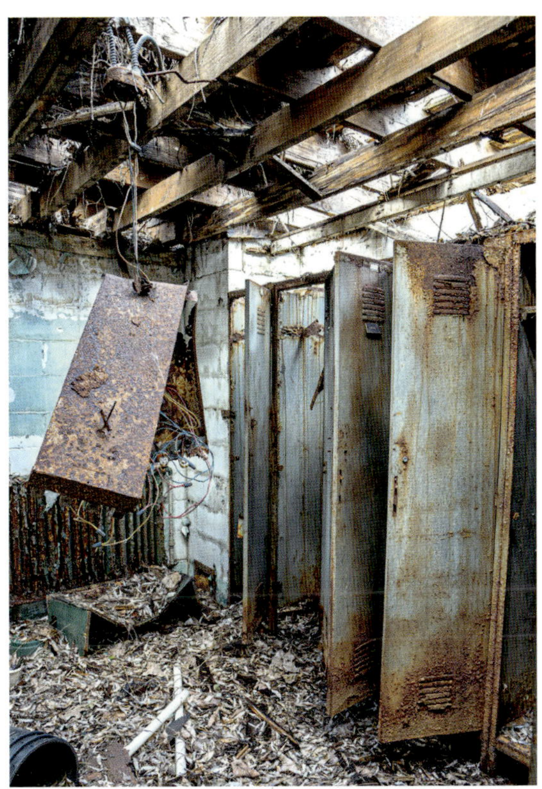

LOCKER ROOM: In the 1950s and 1960s, large freeways were constructed around the greenhouse site.

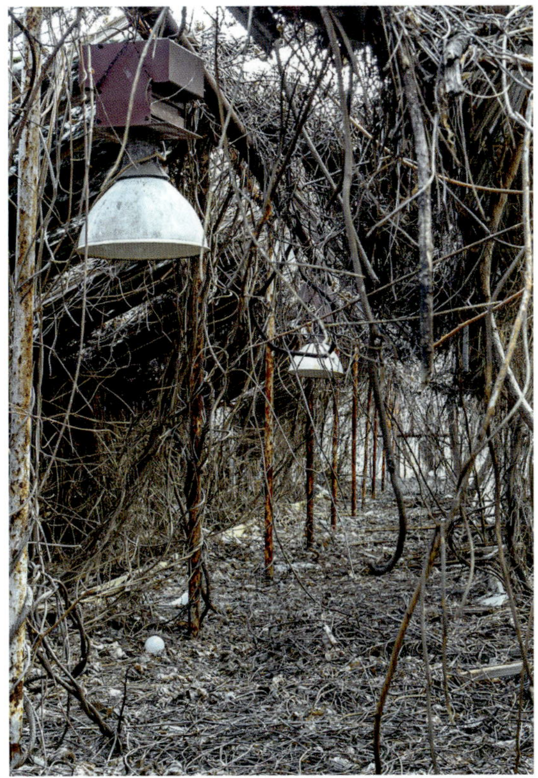

HOT HOUSE INTERIOR: The nurseries and greenhouses that supported the U.S. Botanic Garden and Capitol cultivated more than 13,000 plants for exhibition, study, and exchange with other institutions.

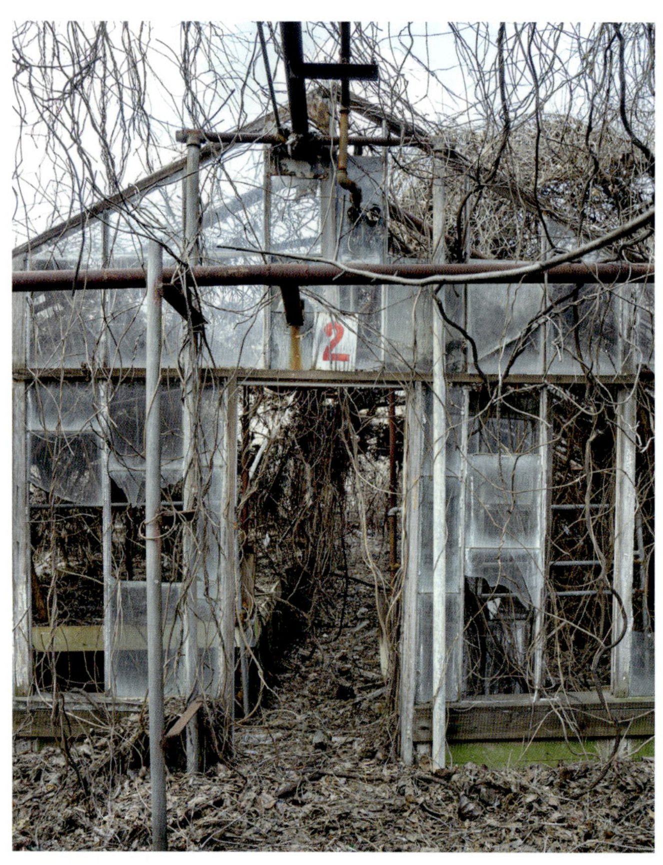

▲ **GREENHOUSE ENTRANCE:** The nursery and greenhouse collections included carnivorous plants, orchids, bromeliads, cacti and succulents, cycads, ferns, and medicinal plants.

▼ **HOTHOUSE AND NURSERY ADMINISTRATION BUILDINGS:** A U.S. Exploratory Expedition departed in 1838 in search of new plant species.

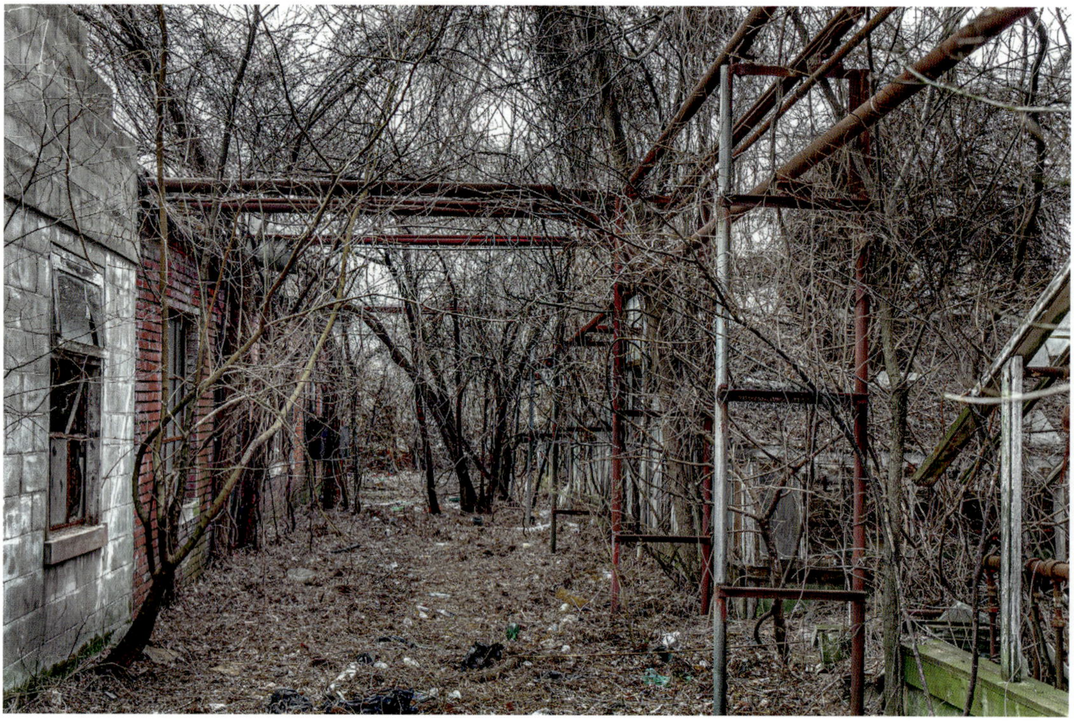

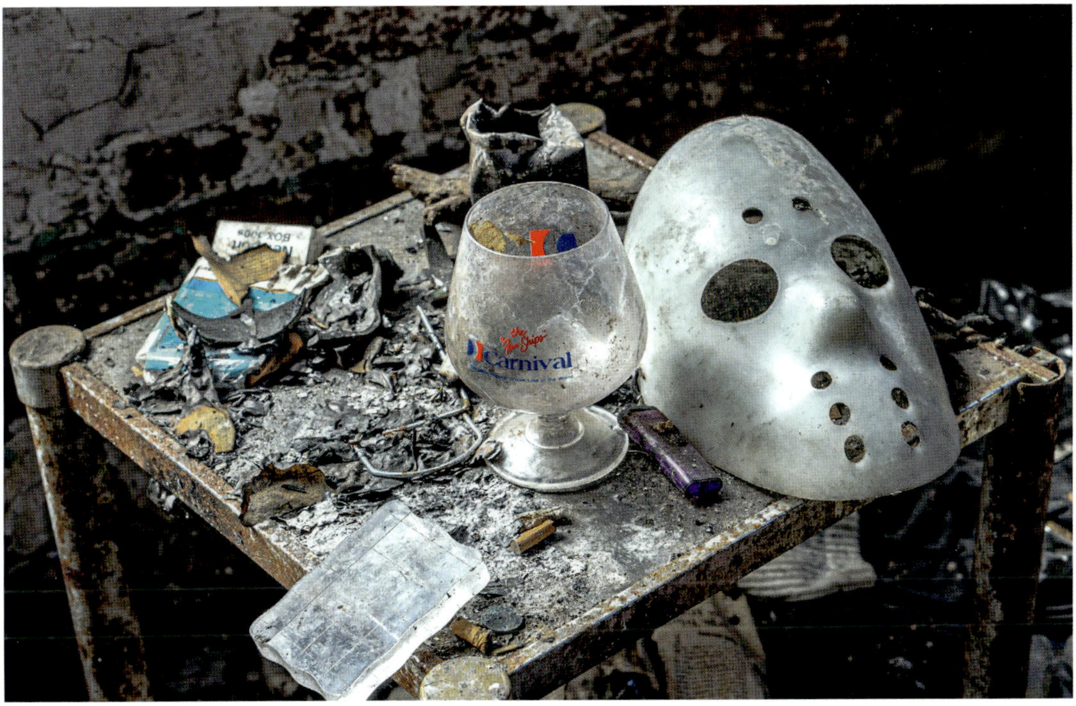

CURIOUS FIND: The greenhouses sheltering and propagating plants joined with the U.S. Botanic Garden in the 1850s when Congress issued appropriations for the construction of such facilities.

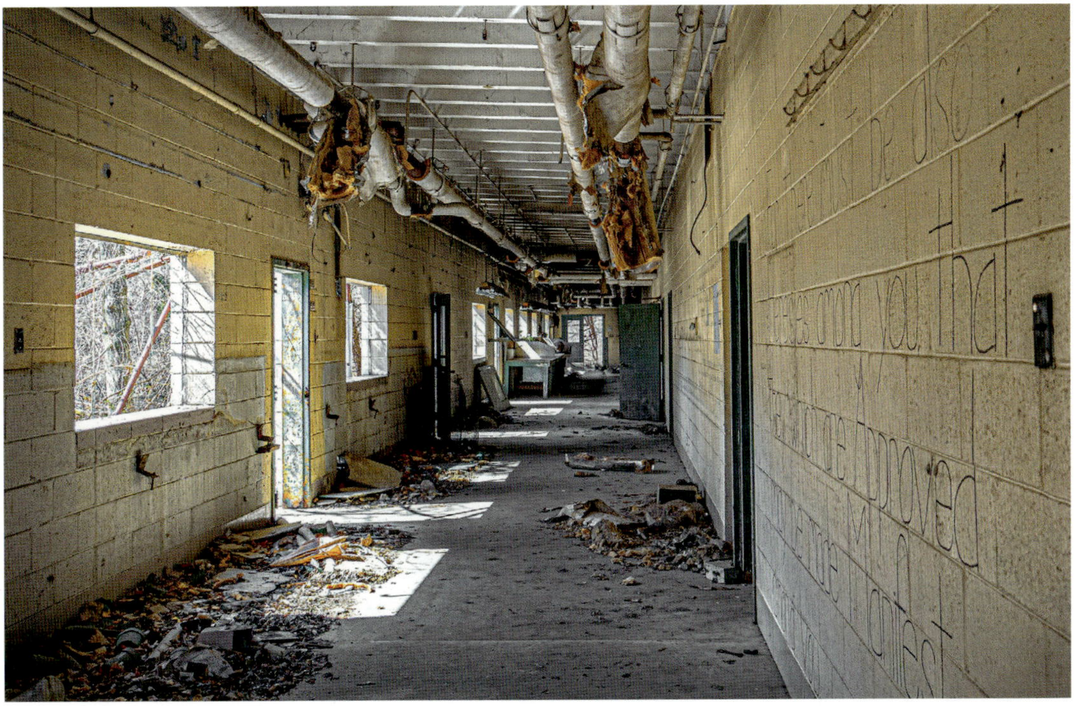

PRODUCTION BUILDING: This site included twenty-four greenhouses in support of the Botanic Garden.

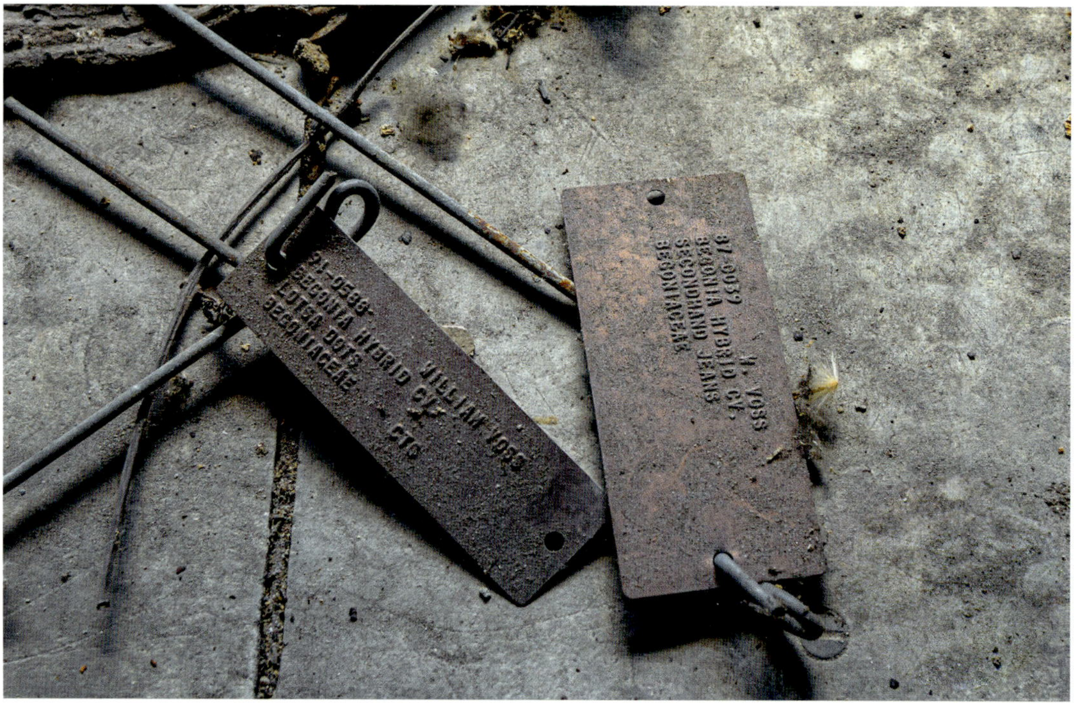

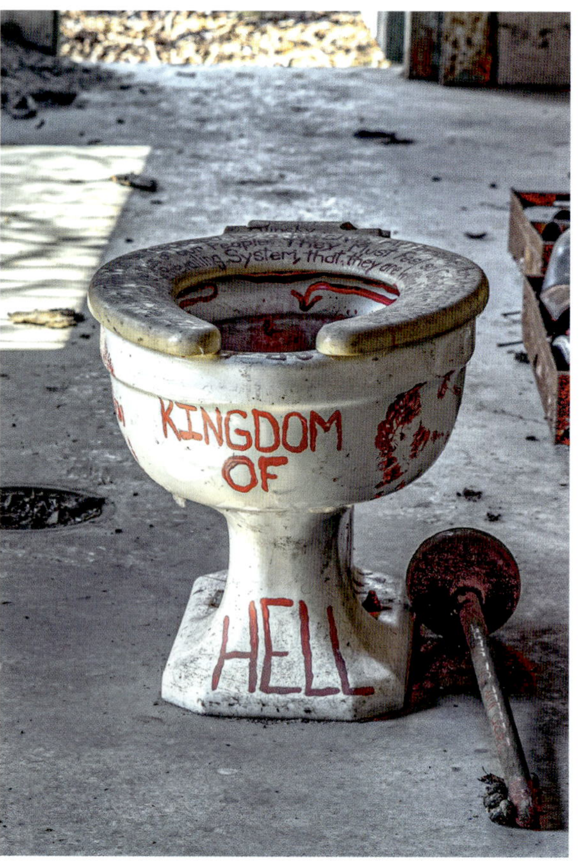

▲ **NURSERY TAGS:** All plants are tagged with plant scientific name, common name, description, range, and source.

▼ **FREE EXPRESSION:** In the 1980s, this site was traded to the Washington Metropolitan Area Transit Authority for construction of a subway station, in exchange for replacement nursery and greenhouse production facilities on 25 acres, four miles away.

7

AN ARTFUL SPIRIT

At first sight, the church-like structure at the crest of a dead-end road in a Southwest Washington, D.C. neighborhood seemed like a psychedelic relic from the 1960s counterculture. The continuous stream of vibrant paint colors and swirly patterns jacketing the building's exterior demands attention. This former historic church is home to Culture House—an urban arts facility featuring a gallery and event venue. I recently drove past this colorful landmark during the time of COVID-19, and Culture House seemed abandoned once again because of some random graffiti scarring the colorful exterior artwork and the unkempt appearance of the property. Especially concerning is a real estate banner affixed to the former church's side. Is Culture House for sale? I am a bit reassured that this artful gem is still very much alive because the Culture House website notes closure due to COVID. Still, that real estate banner in full view appears sticky, but perhaps, the banner is only a source for space leasing within the eccentric structure. I remain optimistic that Culture House is healthy and merely taking a siesta during the pandemic.

Culture House has origins with the Friendship Baptist Church ("Friendship"). Friendship was once an essential keystone for the collective unity of this Southwest neighborhood; it served its congregation for nearly a century. Constructed in 1886 by former slaves, Friendship is one of the oldest surviving buildings within this region of D.C.'s footprint.

In the 1950s, Washington D.C. urban planners viewed the Southwest community as blighted and, thus, razed most of the structures. While not much survived the wrath of the wrecking ball, Friendship escaped demolition. With the D.C. Redevelopment Land Agency acquiring almost ninety-nine percent of the Southwest neighborhood, it is remarkable that Friendship still stood among the vacant lots. Nevertheless, in short order, Friendship's congregation outgrew its space and relocated to a larger site. The former Friendship realized ownership changes several times until it finally shuttered in 2001.

With the abandoned Friendship achieving D.C. Historic Site status, and the D.C. Historic Preservation Board keeping a watch on any development plans for Friendship, a developer's plans to convert the church into a mixed-use facility of condominiums and offices were overruled by the Preservation Board. The Preservation Board's strong-arm prevented Friendship from having its architectural and historical essence radically altered. The rejected developer, however, submitted alternate plans for the structure to include a vision directed toward an arts-based use. Hence, Culture House, originally monikered Blind Whino for a short period, was born.

The developer commissioned Atlanta-based contemporary artist, Alex Brewer, known as Hense, to design a vibrant exterior coat. A lively multicolor pattern envelopes the former church's façade. The interior is equally buoyant and colorful, with the nave converted into a vivacious performance venue. With more than 15,000 square feet, Culture House provides an eclectic setting for D.C. events, including wedding receptions, stage performances, and private and corporate events. Additionally, much of the interior space is devoted to art galleries and art exhibits.

Culture House fits quite well within this neighborhood's evolving creative personality. The Southwest area is quickly turning into an arts and entertainment quarter with several new performance venues, restaurants, and galleries joining the party. The former Friendship Baptist Church held a religious and civic spirit, and its transformation into Culture House indeed holds a new kind of spirit for service to its community.

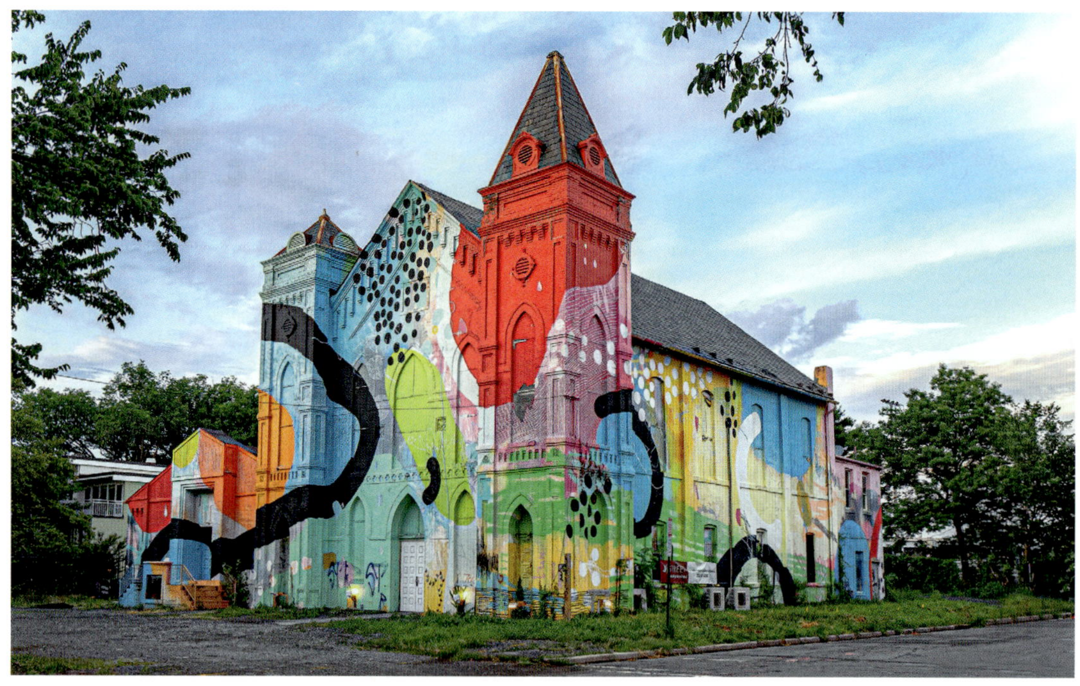

CULTURE HOUSE: A former historic Baptist church and one of the oldest structures in Southwest D.C. is now Culture House—an arts collective.

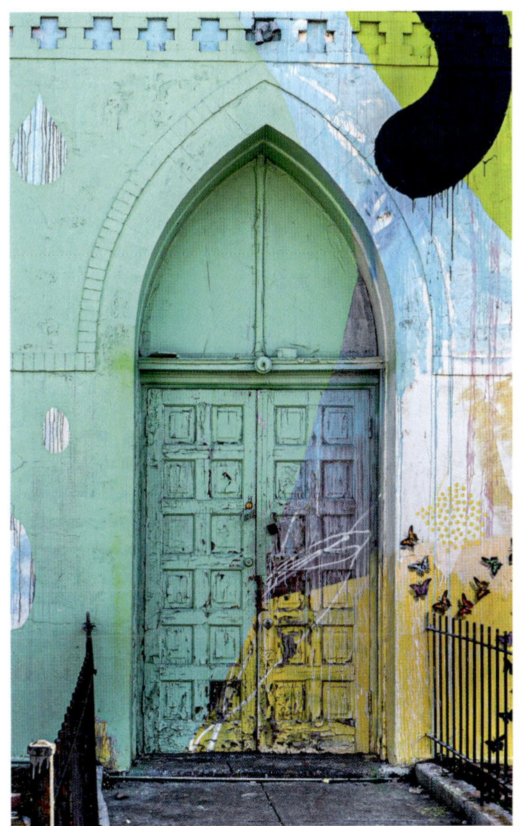

ENTRANCE: The former church was eventually repurposed into an arts facility and, for a time before its moniker, Culture House, was The Blind Whino.

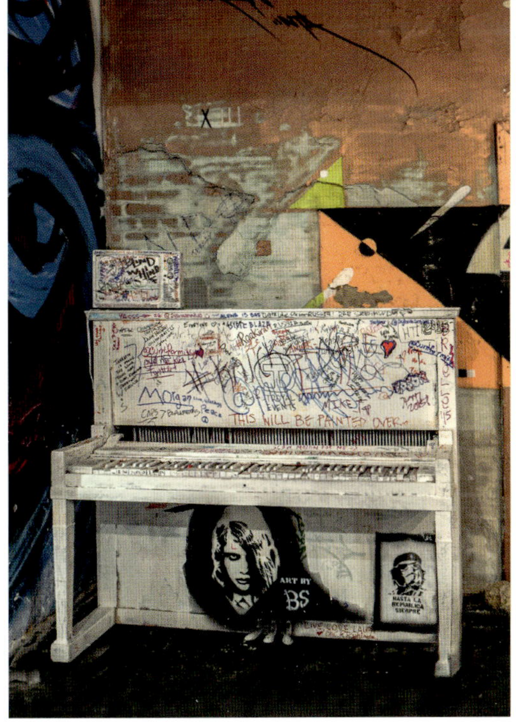

REPURPOSED PIANO: Atlanta painter, Hense, painted the exterior of the former church.

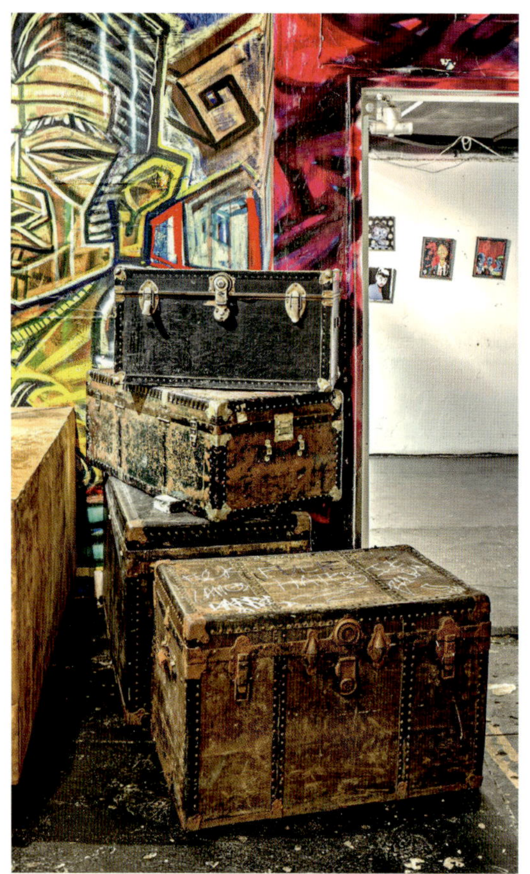

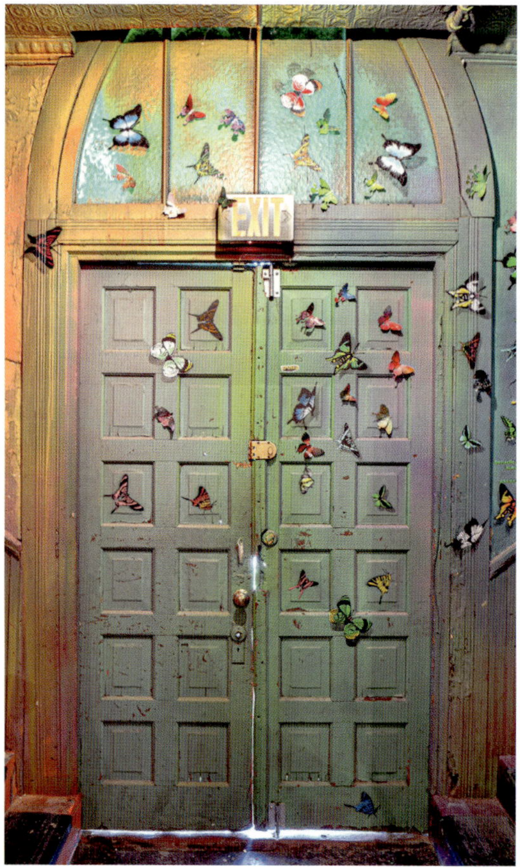

◀ **ART GALLERY IN REAR AND REPURPOSED ARTIFACTS:** Culture House holds a performance venue as well as a gallery annex for art exhibits.

▶ **EXIT:** Culture House was built in 1886 by former slaves.

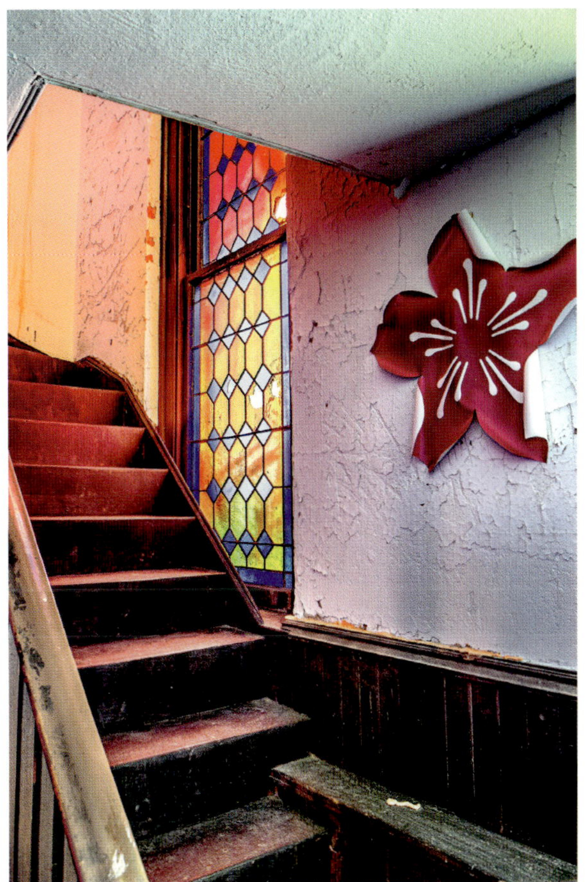

▲ **STAIRCASE AND PRESERVED STAINED GLASS:** The D.C. Historic Preservation Board prevented the site from conversion into condominiums and office space.

▼ **FORMER CHURCH NAVE AS AN EVENT VENUE:** The bold exterior color and style also flows into the interior of Culture House.

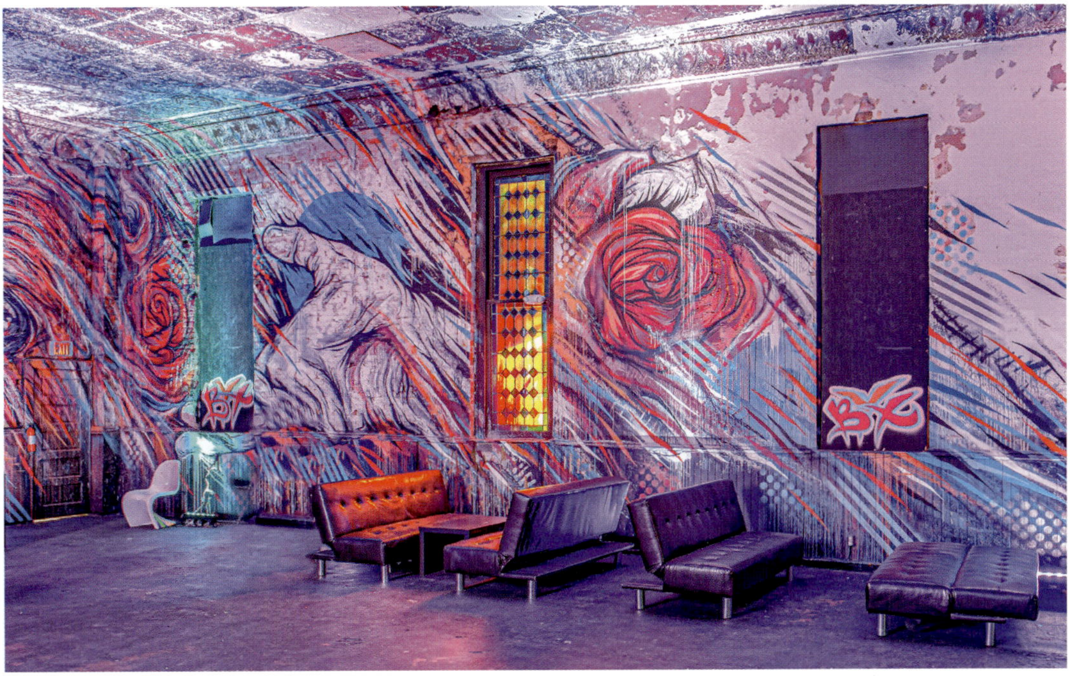

8

LEST WE FORGET

Downtown D.C. holds endless historical landmarks and museums with every glance and stone's throw. A bit removed from the National Mall's monuments and essential archival depositories, though, one finds additional art stockpiles in D.C.'s centuries-old cemeteries. I always viewed graveyards as beautiful and peaceful chronicled reserves, concurrently solemn and loving, and this cemetery, Congressional, was not an exception.

For more than two centuries, D.C.'s historic Congressional Cemetery ("Congressional") was a final resting site for many famous Washingtonians. In its infancy, the graveyard was attached to the U.S. Congress and was, in fact, the United States' first national cemetery before Arlington National Cemetery's debut in the late 1860s. By the 1830s, almost all Congressmen passing away within the District were interred in Congressional Cemetery. In 1820, burial privileges extended to the families of Congressmen and other government officials. From Congressional's rooting, Christ Church continues to keep watch over the cemetery.

Congressional, however, encountered neglect in the twentieth century. With unruly grass, invasive vines, rampant weeds, upset headstones, damaged monuments, ample litter, as well as specters of street danger lurking in the dark, Congressional appeared abandoned, and in essence, was abandoned, because no one seemed to care about it. Still, a local group valued the cemetery and thought it was worth saving. An unwritten neighborhood tradition allowed dog owners to walk their pets through Congressional and permit them to run freely within the cemetery's gated confines. This group of Congressional dog-walkers decided to tax themselves, with said taxes allocated for cemetery ground maintenance. The group evolved into the K9 Corps at Historic Congressional Cemetery, holding to a long list of members contributing annual fees for the privilege of walking their dogs off-leash through Congressional. The K9 Corps saved the site from further neglect and brought forth greater interest in the preservation of Congressional. Private donations, some congressional appropriations, foundation grants, and thousands of volunteers from school, church, and military groups direct contributions toward the maintenance and security of Congressional.

While Congressional's landscape still looks a little shopworn, with some areas in need of a string trimmer and several monuments and headstones silently shouting for repair and restoration, the graveyard is thriving, active, and finally a National Historic Landmark. Like any lifecycle, human-made structures and sites need increasing attention too. Nothing lasts on its own, and this tenet applies to beings as well as human-made monuments. A name on a memorial assumes continuity of lineage, but even the names on stones fade without a regular watch directed toward preservation. Community activism built a new track for Congressional to steer its heritage toward posterity.

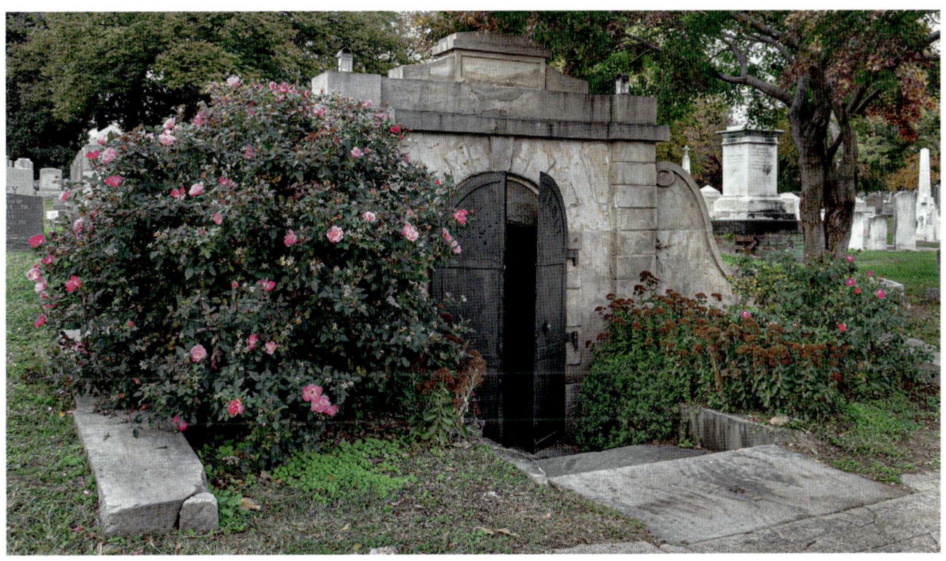

PUBLIC VAULT: The Public Vault, constructed in 1832-34, with funds appropriated by Congress, temporarily stored bodies before burial.

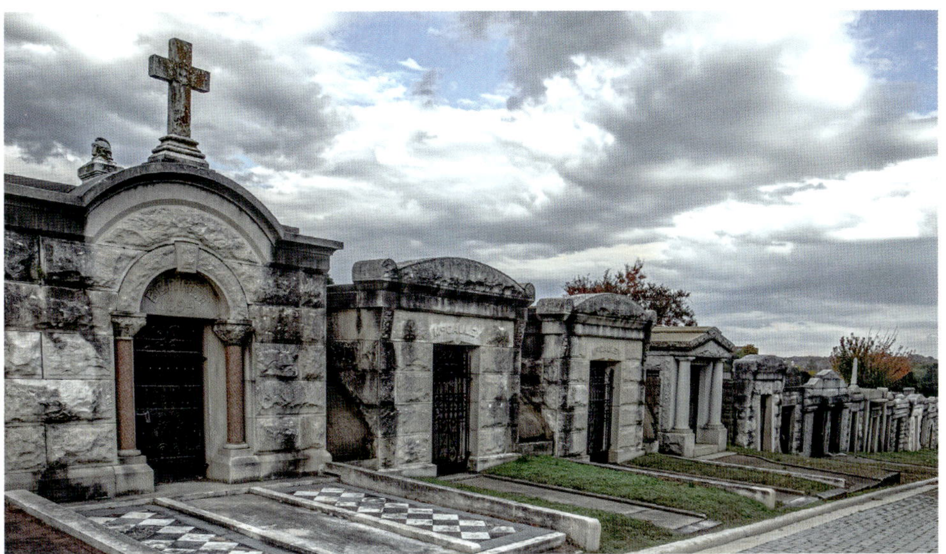

MAUSOLEUM ROW: Vestibule type mausoleums hold doorways for entry. Often, a small chapel is inside mausoleums.

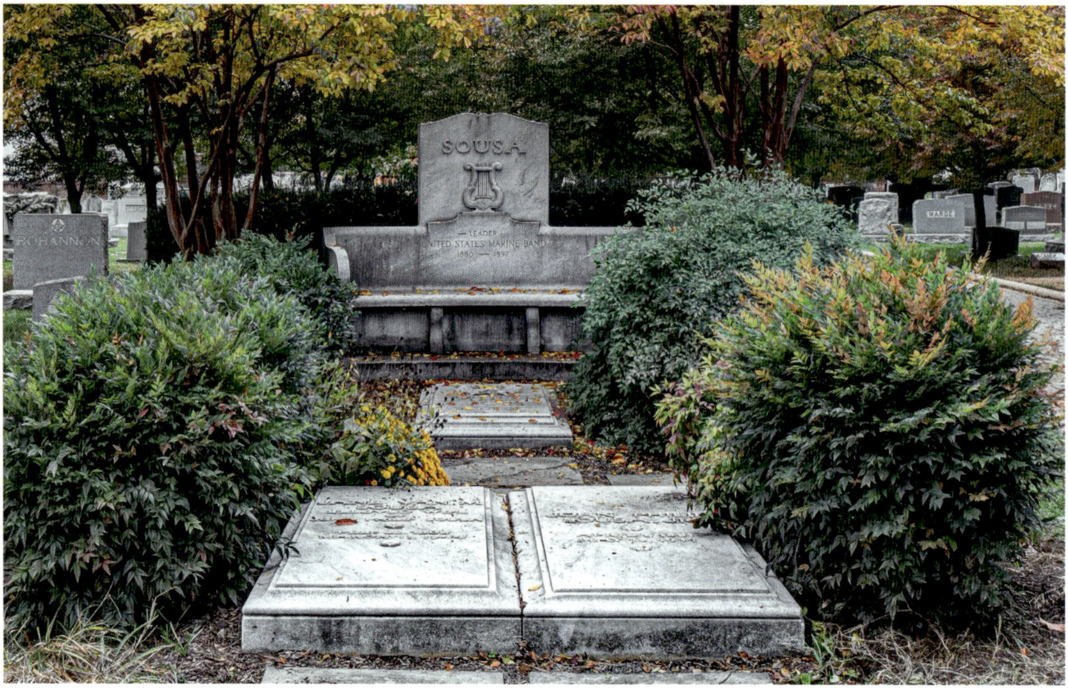

JOHN PHILIP SOUZA'S GRAVE: Souza spent part of his life in Washington, D.C. Each November 6, Souza's birthday, Congressional Cemetery honors the conductor/composer with a graveside Marine Corp band concert.

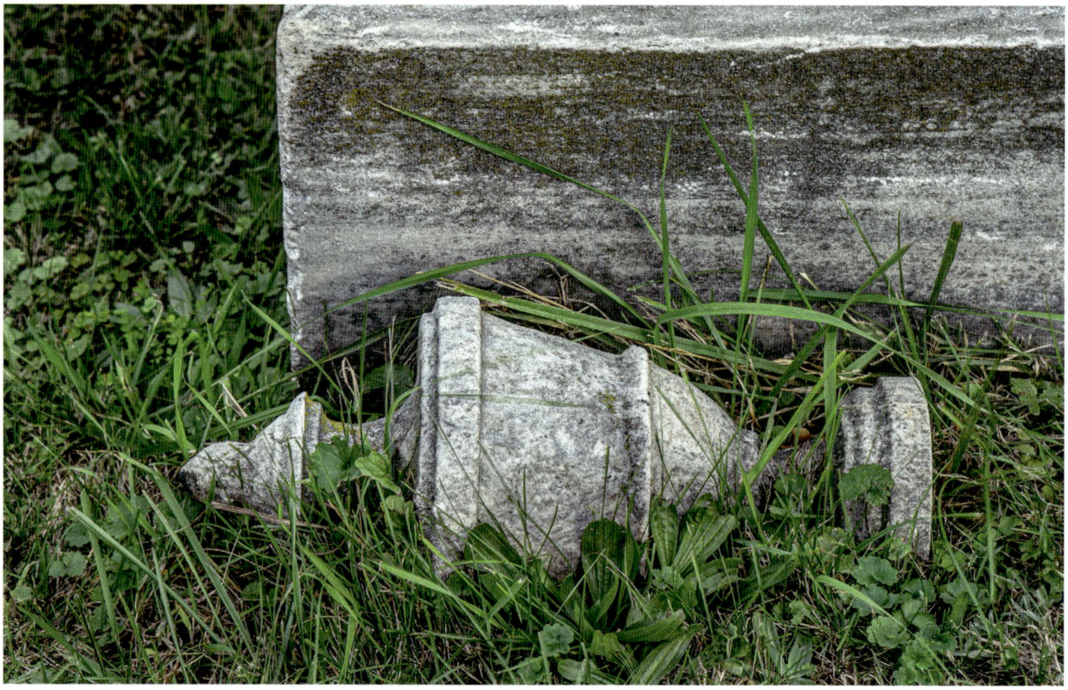

BROKEN MONUMENT: Congressional Cemetery is not government property. Since 1976, the Episcopal church, Christ Church, maintained a close relationship with the cemetery's managing nonprofit group, Association for the Preservation of Historic Congressional Cemetery.

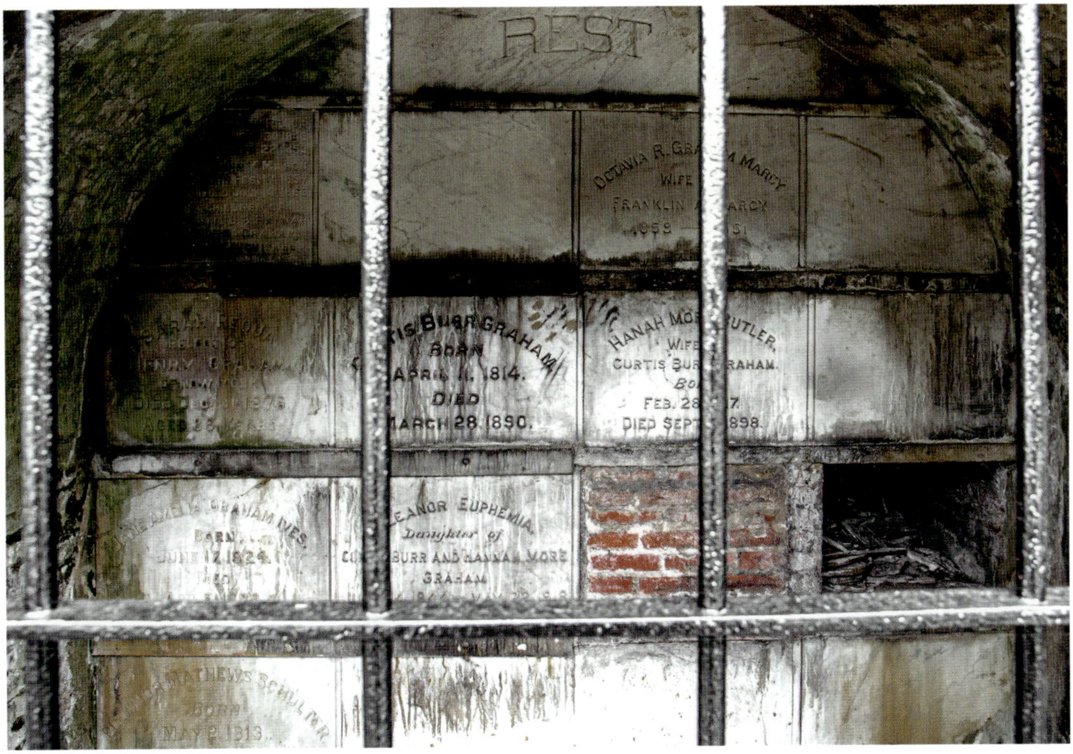

▲ **VANDALIZED VAULT:** So neglected and forgotten, that by 1997, Congressional Cemetery joined the National Trust for Historic Preservation's list of the most endangered historic sites.

▼ **MAUSOLEUM PLAQUE INSCRIPTION - "INEXORABLE DEATH'S DOINGS":** This mausoleum, built in 1835, holds sixteen—some connected to the famous Shriver family. After years of neglect and vandalism, the tomb was restored.

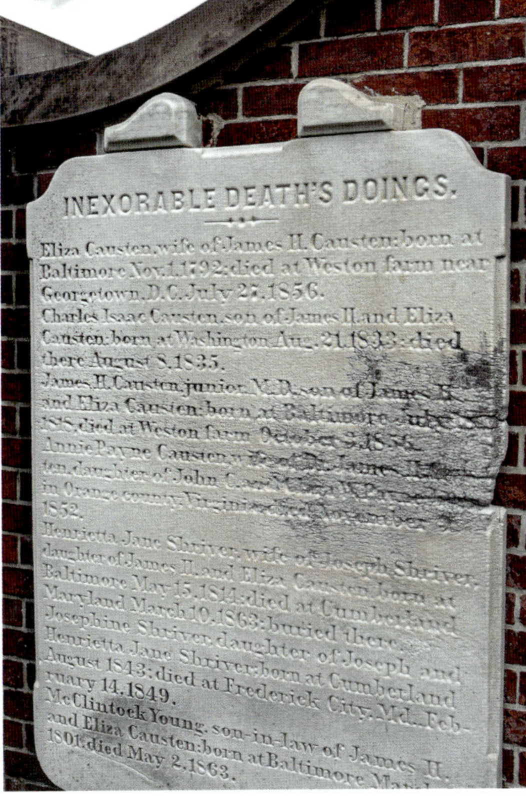

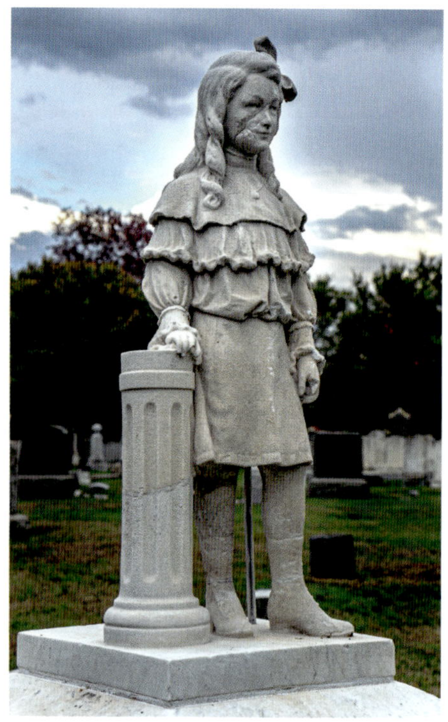

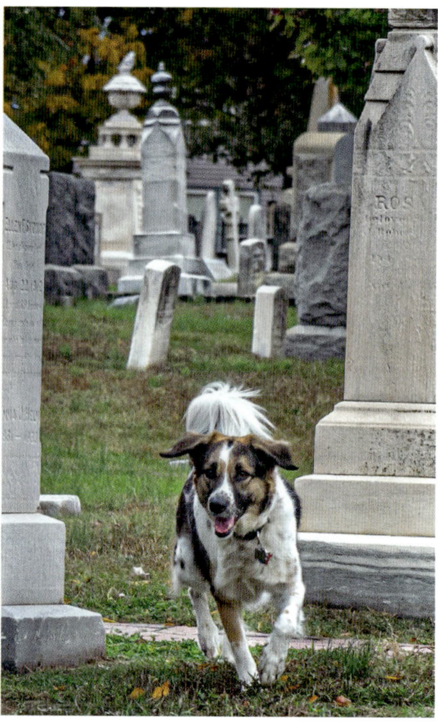

◄ **MARION OOLETIA KAHLERT MONUMENT:** This monument was vandalized in the 1980s and restored in 2010 via public donations. The monument's column is short, representing Marion's short life. One account has Marion as the first automobile fatality in D.C., but another claims Marion succumbed to kidney failure at ten years old.

► **HAPPY VISITOR:** Congressional cemetery receives approximately twenty-five percent of its operating income from its dog-walking program, the K9 Corp.

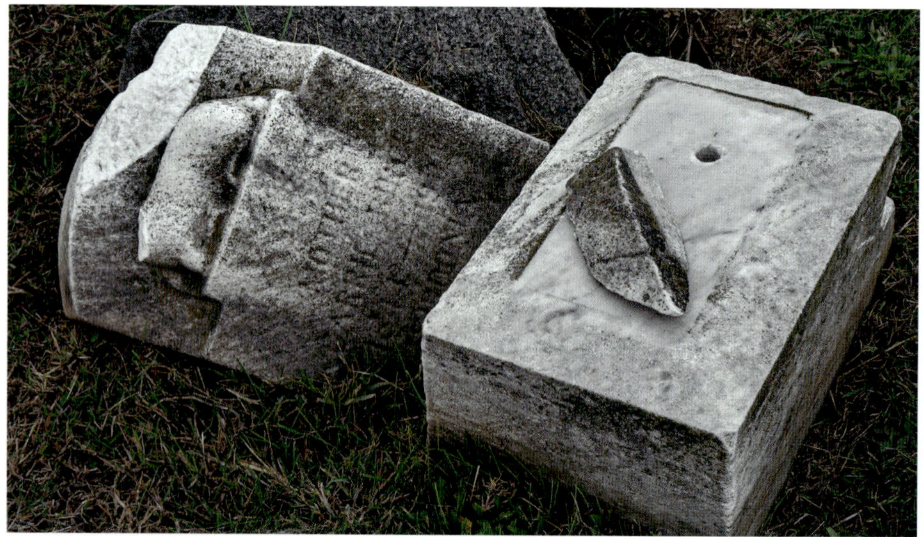

BROKEN MARKER: In 2015, goats were introduced to the cemetery, courtesy of an anonymous donor, to control invasive species, such as poison ivy, kudzu, English ivy, and poison sumac.

9

SCHOOL'S OUT

Many of Washington, D.C.'s schools were built when public education was held in high esteem—as a path to personal enrichment. The history of D.C.'s public schools followed the city's growth trajectory in the 1800s. When D.C. established a department to supervise public education in 1804, the City had only become the nexus of the federal government a few years prior. Many accepted the belief that public schools leveled cultural differences by amalgamating generations of immigrants and ultimately integrating African Americans into American society.

Two main historical elements appeared within D.C.'s public school early development—the separation of races into separate educational facilities and the separation of sexes. African-American schools advanced in 1807 by way of private citizenry sponsorship and religious group endeavors. In 1862, Congress provided for the creation of public schools for African-American students. At the twilight of the Civil War, a new era in school construction commenced. The public was committed to public education and desired better schools. Additionally, the federal government wanted to showcase its status and power and elevate D.C. as the capital of a grand unified Republic. D.C.'s population expanded by a factor of two from 1860 to 1870 due to an inflow of freed slaves from the South, as well as Northerners relocating to this area. The need for services and infrastructure was a priority of the government's planning agenda.

Until 1954, the District's public schools were segregated by law. With Brown v. Board of Education, the Supreme Court declared segregation in schools as unconstitutional. The District desegregated immediately; however, surrounding suburbs and much of the country did not follow suit. During the 1970s and 1980s, the District faced excess school capacity for a reduced student body as a result of a diminishing populace. Shortly thereafter, the budget crisis of the 1990s grew so dire that Congress appointed a Financial Control Board to supervise the City's elected officials and manage the school system. Demographic changes and budget constraints of the past forty years contributed to the shuttering of schools.

Unfortunately, an abundance of abandoned schools dot the District landscape. The days of school overcrowding are no longer realities, with some schools repurposed, and some renovated into residential condominiums or office space. A few schools hold rich histories and await second chances for new lives. Public schools anchor their neighborhoods and turn children into responsible citizens, and it is troubling to view so many centers of learning not fulfilling the promise of original intent. School is out, as are so many learning opportunities.

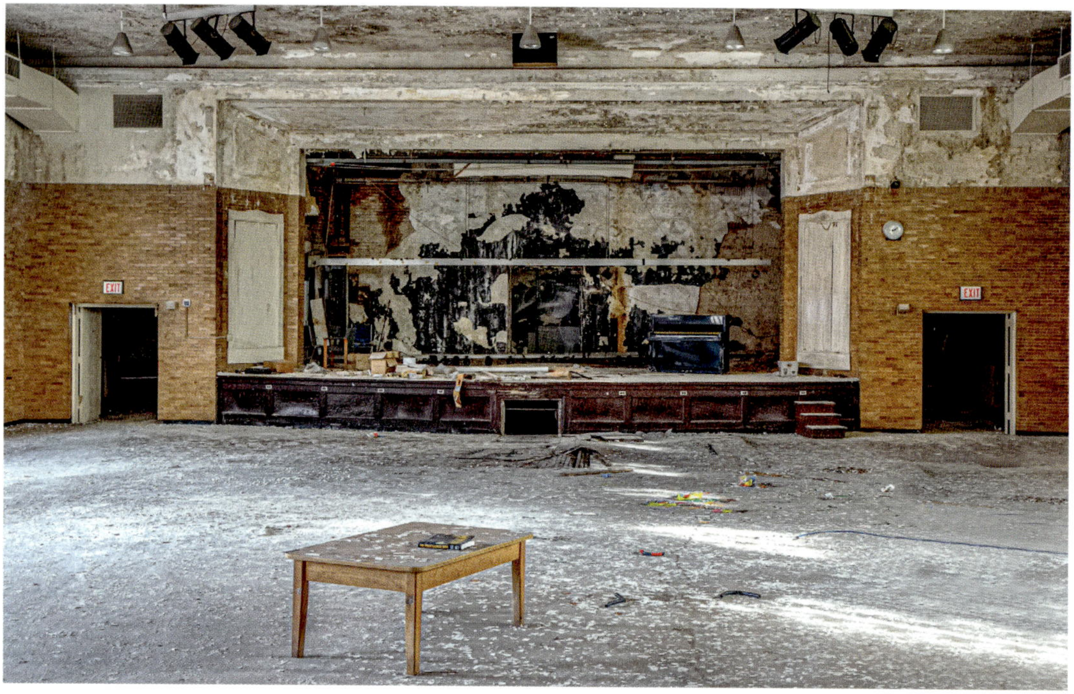

AUDITORIUM: Established in 1906 but abandoned since 1978, this school converted from an elementary school to a junior high school in 1927 and expanded to meet Southwest D.C.'s African American community's educational demands.

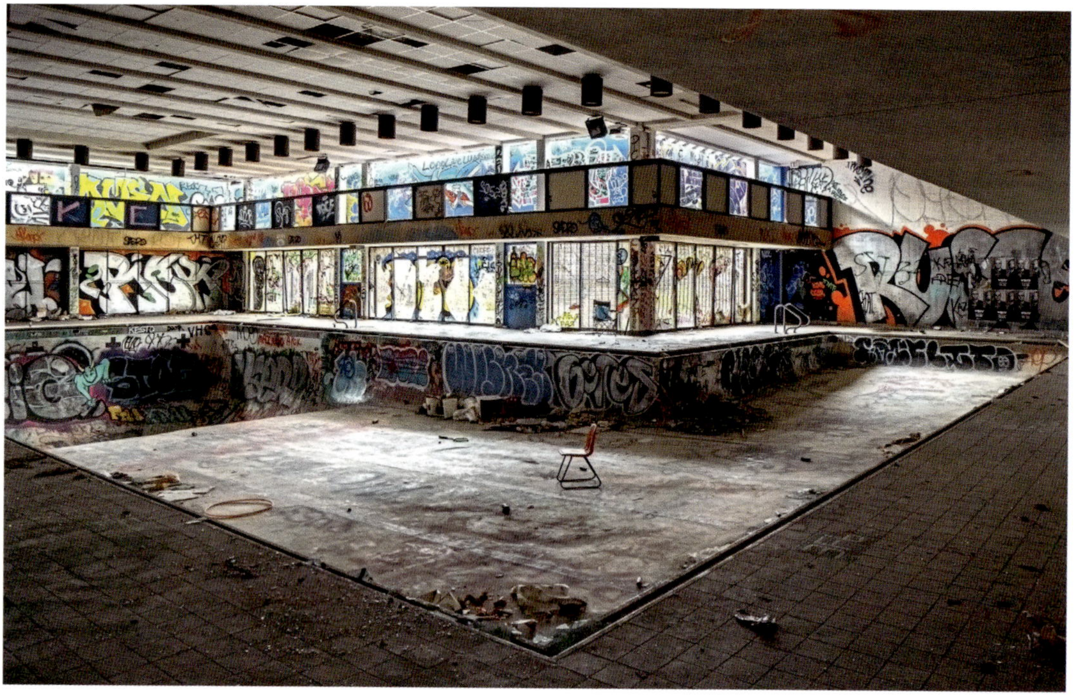

INDOOR POOL: The Washington, D.C. public school system commenced in 1804, but did not name schools for people until 1864.

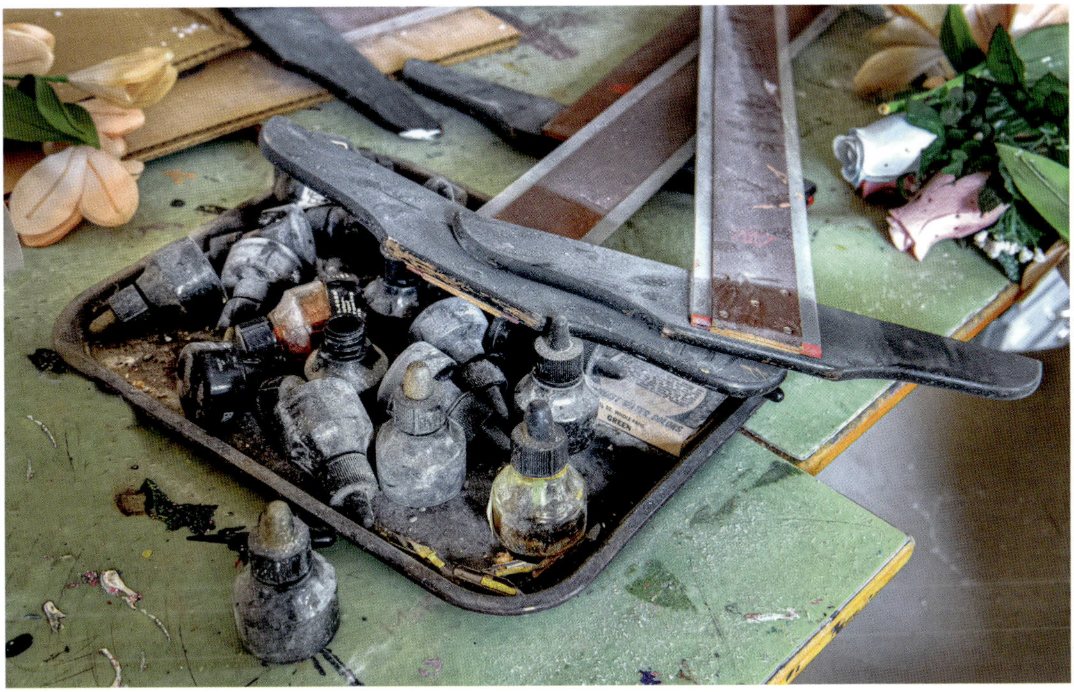

ARTS ROOM: In addition to naming schools for presidents, D.C. chief executives joined the school naming list during the late nineteenth and early twentieth century.

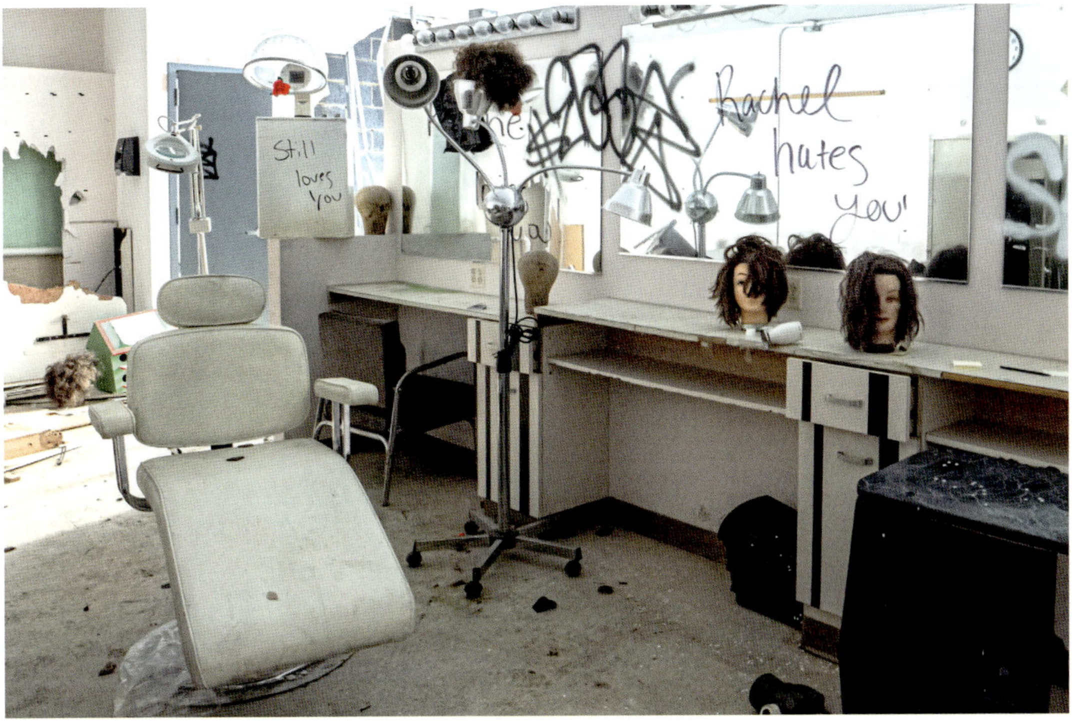

COSMETOLOGY AND HAIR STYLING ROOM: In the twentieth century, the school board modified its school naming philosophy with several schools named for teachers, principals, superintendents, and school board members.

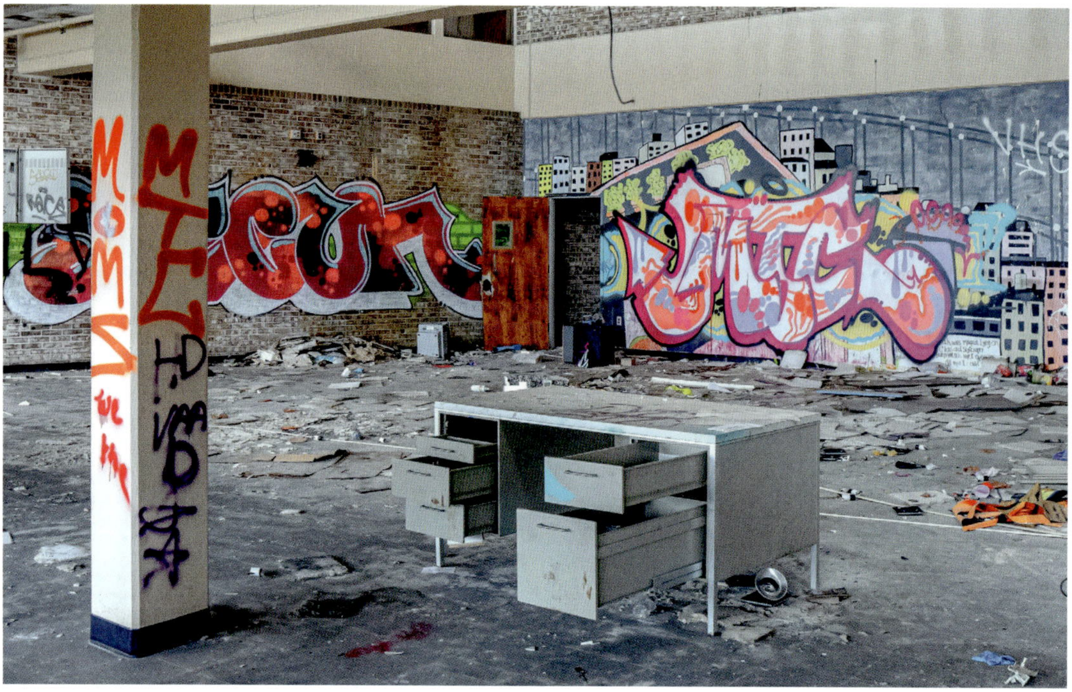

OPEN CONCEPT CLASSROOM: An older school is not likely to meet the classroom size, support spaces, or large spaces for modern educational demands.

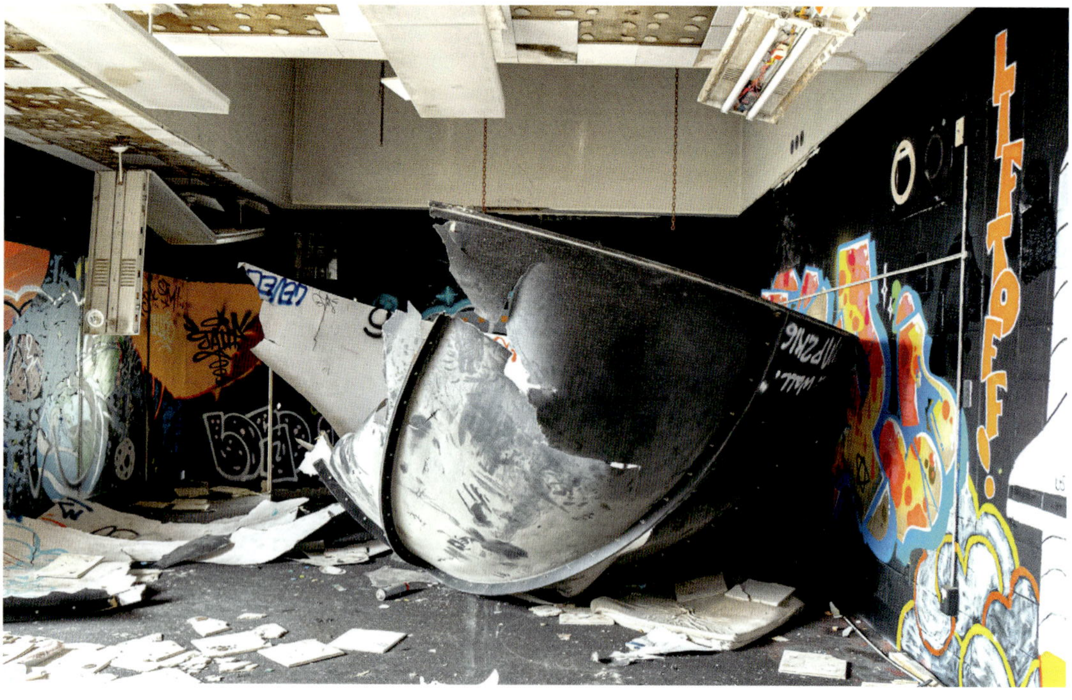

PLANETARIUM DOME: There are two D.C. schools named for people attached to the Confederacy: Tyler, named for former President Tyler, who led the Virginia Secession movement; and D.C. Mayor Walter Lenox, who joined the Confederate Army.

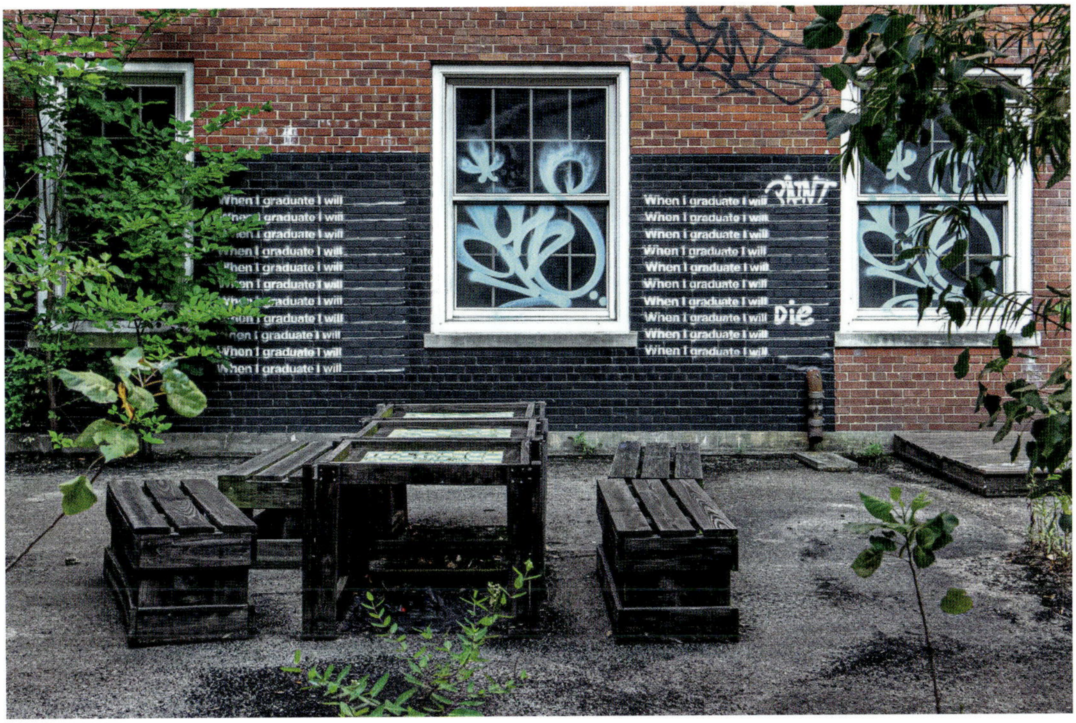

▲ **COURTYARD:** D.C.'s twentieth-century public school served a broader range of educational purposes than that of the previous century because of a more diverse population, as well as the inclusion of more programs such as industrial, vocational, and business education.

▼ **SCIENCE LAB:** A 1998 Army Corps of Engineering assessment noted that seventy percent of D.C.'s school buildings were in poor physical condition.

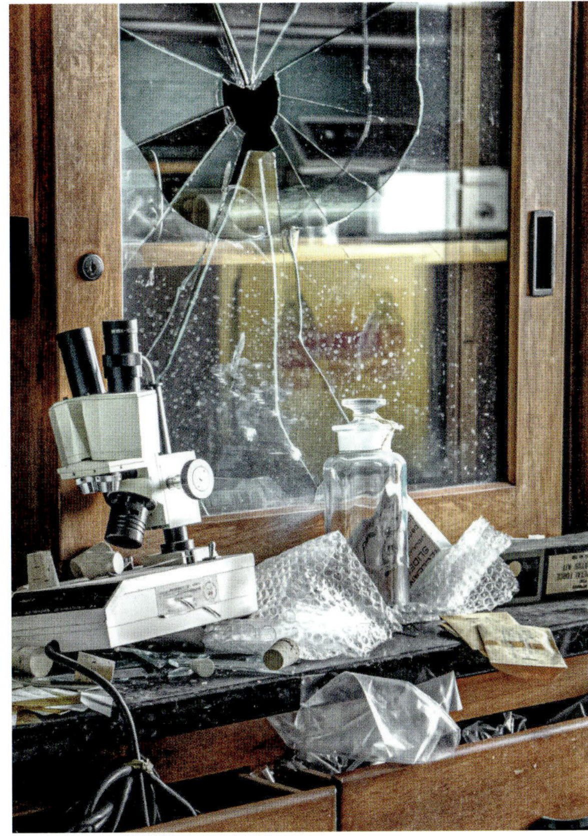

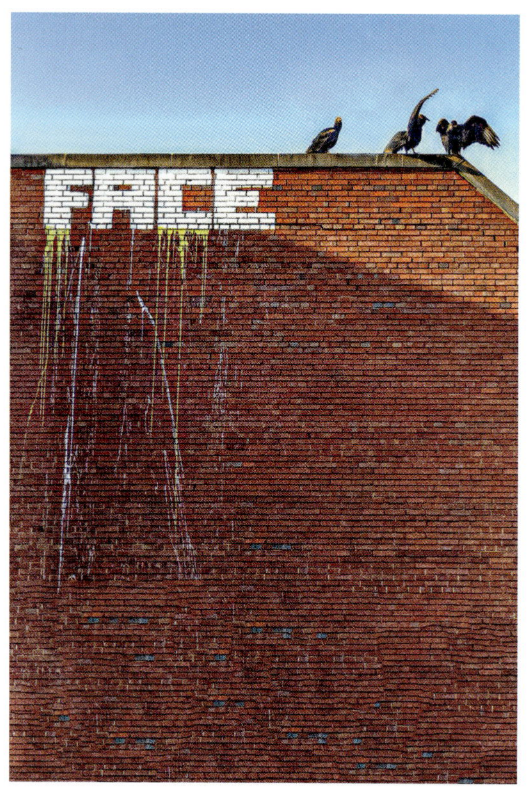

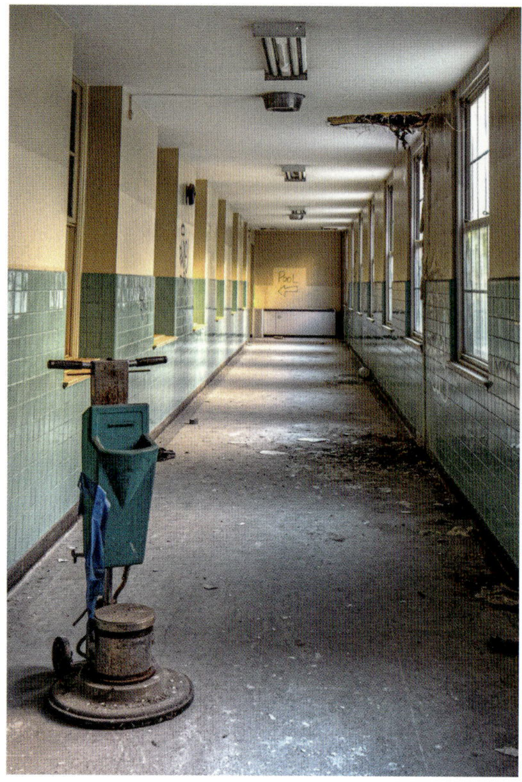

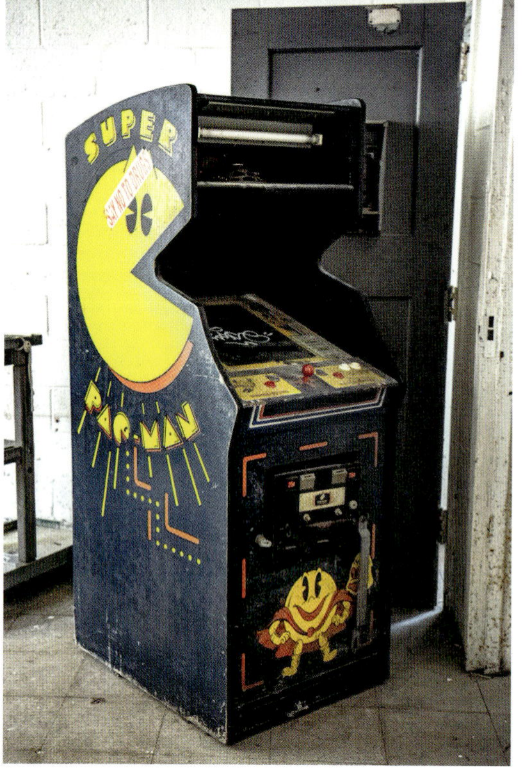

▲ **SCHOOL FACE GRAFFITI:** In 1948, most high school curriculums included a band, orchestra, choral group, and music appreciation. Today, only six high schools have a band, and none have orchestras.

▲ **HALLWAY:** Half of the District's middle-level schools do not have a vocational education teacher, one-third are without an art teacher, and one-third are absent a music teacher.

▼ **PACMAN:** Overcrowding of schools continued to be a problem throughout the 1930s. Older buildings slated for demolition were kept in service to meet the demand for more classrooms.

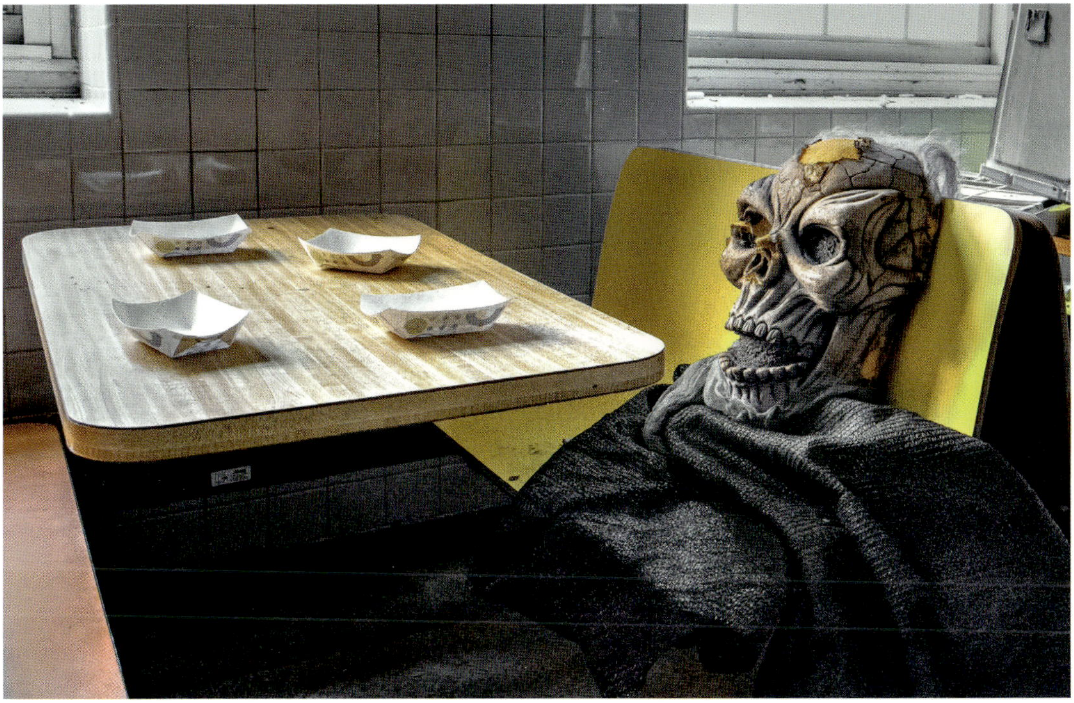

CAFETERIA GUEST: With the advent of World War II, school overcrowding worsened and compounded when schools were used for war effort administration.

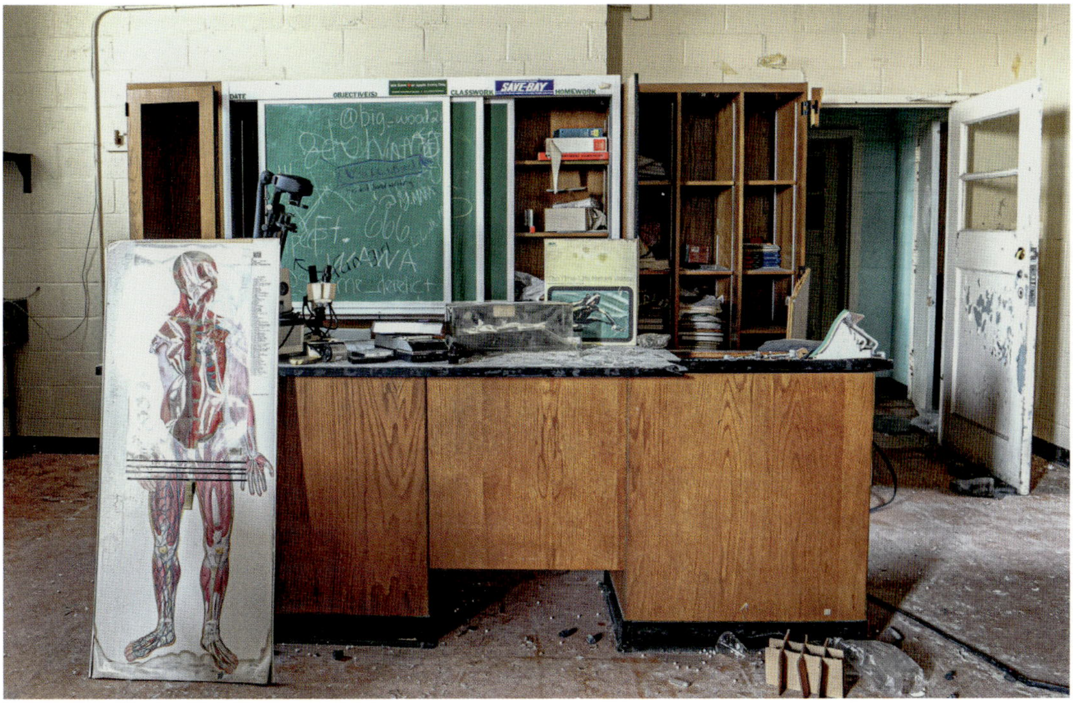

BIOLOGY LAB: The promise of Brown v. Education, and Bolling v. Sharpe, is that every child has equal educational opportunities, but ninety years later, is this a reality?

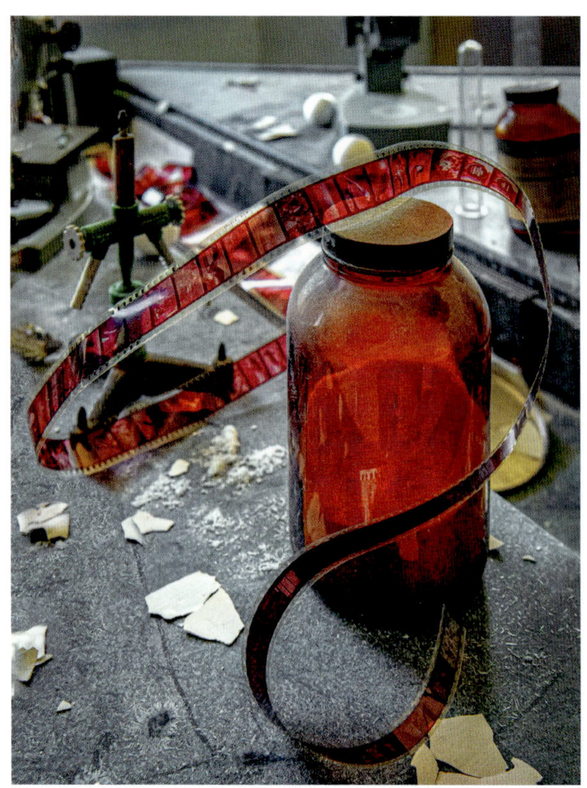

SCIENCE LAB: Until 1954, D.C.'s public schools segregated by law. In Bolling v. Sharpe, a case joining Brown, the Supreme Court acknowledged segregation in D.C. schools as unconstitutional.

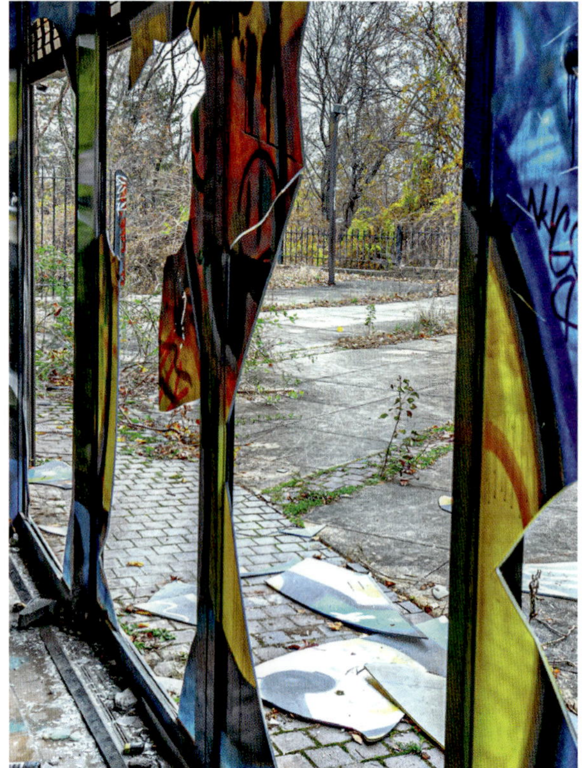

BROKEN DOORS TO COURTYARD: In 2005, over three-quarters of D.C.'s African American students are in schools holding ninety percent of African American demographics.

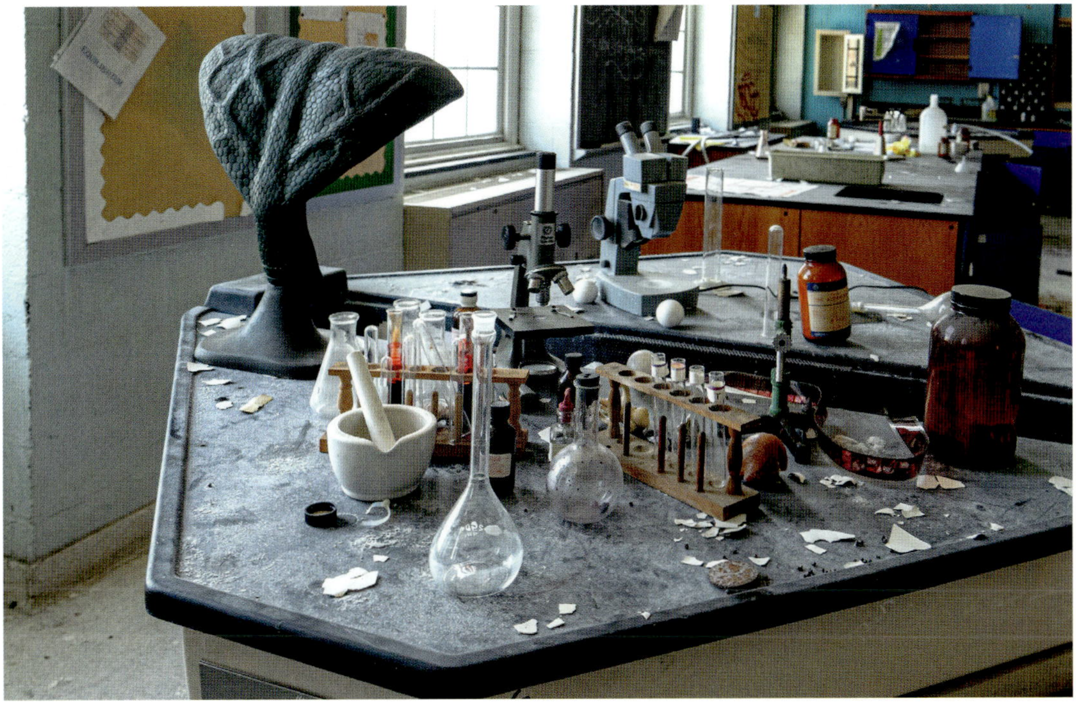

SCIENCE LAB: D.C. schools have a high percentage of students with more significant needs, particularly low-income students.

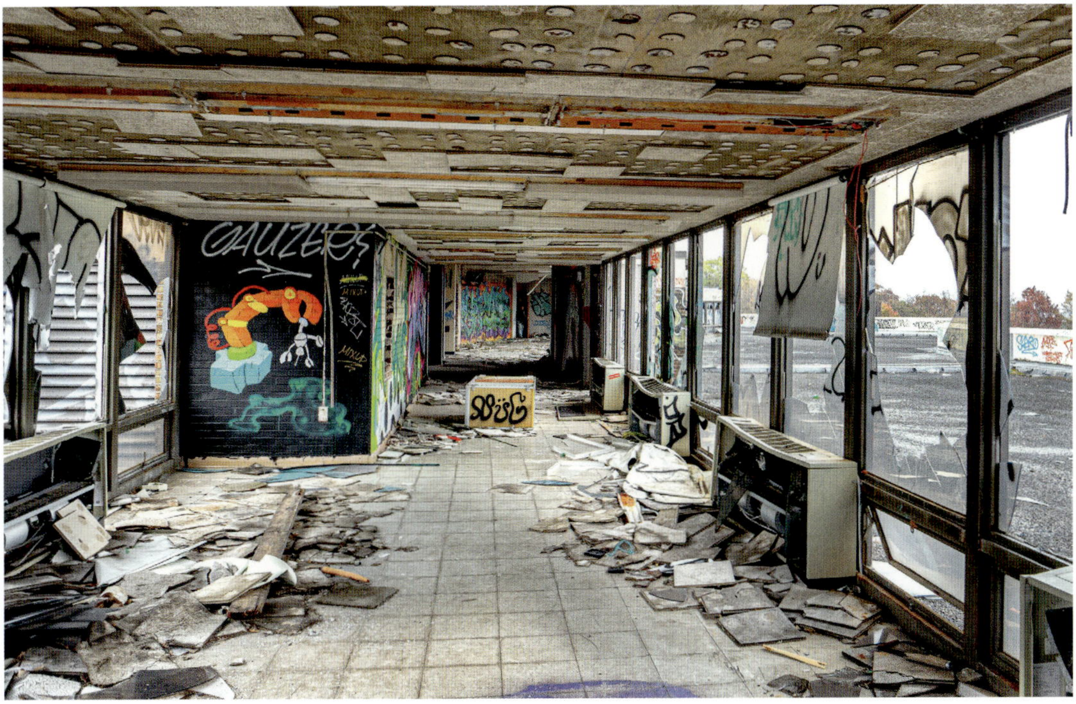

HALLWAY: Since the Brown and Bolling Supreme Court decisions, inequitable education remains a critical problem in the District.

10

DON'T DRINK THE WATER

What are those imposing ivy-covered cylinders sitting on a large tract of fenced land along North Capitol Street? For decades, my curiosity always piqued as I drove by this site. It was not until several years ago, and shortly after I dove headfirst into the urban exploration sub-culture, did I learn the purpose of these abandoned contemporary Stonehenge-like monoliths—the relics of the sidelined McMillan Sand Filtration Site ("McMillan"), a twenty-five-acre decommissioned water treatment complex.

In 1905, McMillan was not only a needed city utility mechanism due to population growth but also the standard for the preservation of D.C. public health. McMillan was instrumental in curbing the typhoid epidemic that engulfed the region at the turn of the twentieth century. The main source of the typhoid problem originated in D.C.'s water supply, where unfiltered water from the Washington Aqueduct held an infestation of bacteria and a copious amount of Potomac River sludge. To alleviate the city's health crisis and the growing demand for more water, the District embarked on an ambitious plan for a new water supply distribution framework. In turn, Congress authorized funding for this new water filtration site.

The new facility, McMillan, used sand to purify water. Raw water came into the facility from the nearby reservoir and slowly percolated through the sand in twenty-five vaulted underground cells before making its way to the taps in D.C. homes and businesses. The four-foot layer of sand in the cells removed bacteria and sediment from the raw water. Large amounts of fresh sand were stored above ground in large concrete cylinders with said sand replacing the top layers when dirt and impurities accumulated. The sand could be shoveled and dropped into the underground cells via 21,000 manholes on the property. When McMillan was completed in 1905, D.C. faced a record year for typhoid, along with water usage of 60,000,000 gallons per day. With filtered water flowing into consumer taps, courtesy of McMillan, the typhoid crisis leveled, and sustained the water needs for the expanding District population. McMillan ceased operations in 1987 and remained abandoned since then.

In 1991, the D.C. Historic Preservation Review Board designated McMillan park as a Historic Landmark and nominated the site for inclusion into the National Register of Historic Places. An advocacy group, McMillan Park Committee, is currently battling development proposals favoring removal of the sand silos and over-commercialization of the property.

Many legal battles about the future use of McMillan ensued over the past decade and have stalled site redevelopment. Public access to the site has been prohibited since World War II, but the site still offers an uncommon, but interesting landscape as well as one steeped in heroic history. McMillian is worthy of a save, not just for historical posterity, but for future generations to have the joy of declaring: what are those big concrete things?

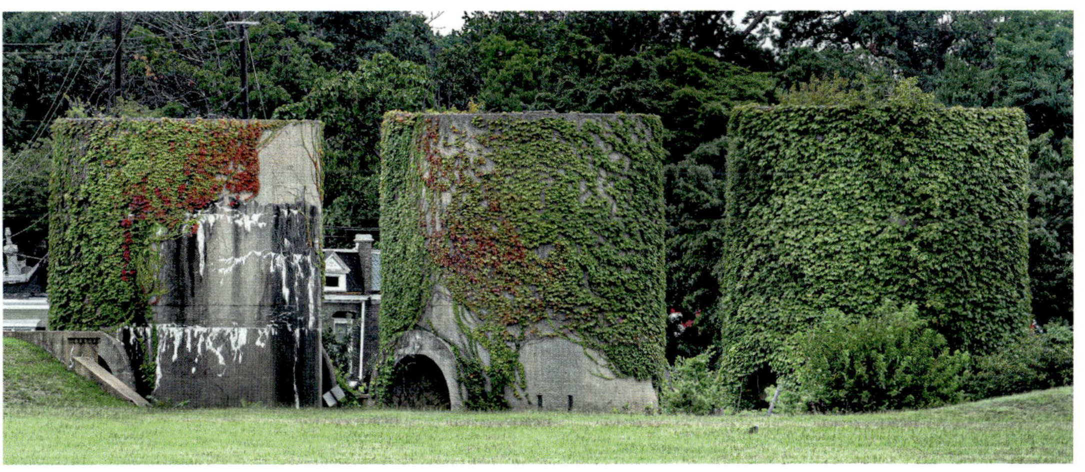

SAND SILO: At the turn of the twentieth century, D.C. was gripped by a typhoid epidemic due, in part, to polluted, unfiltered water carried to homes and businesses from the Washington Aqueduct.

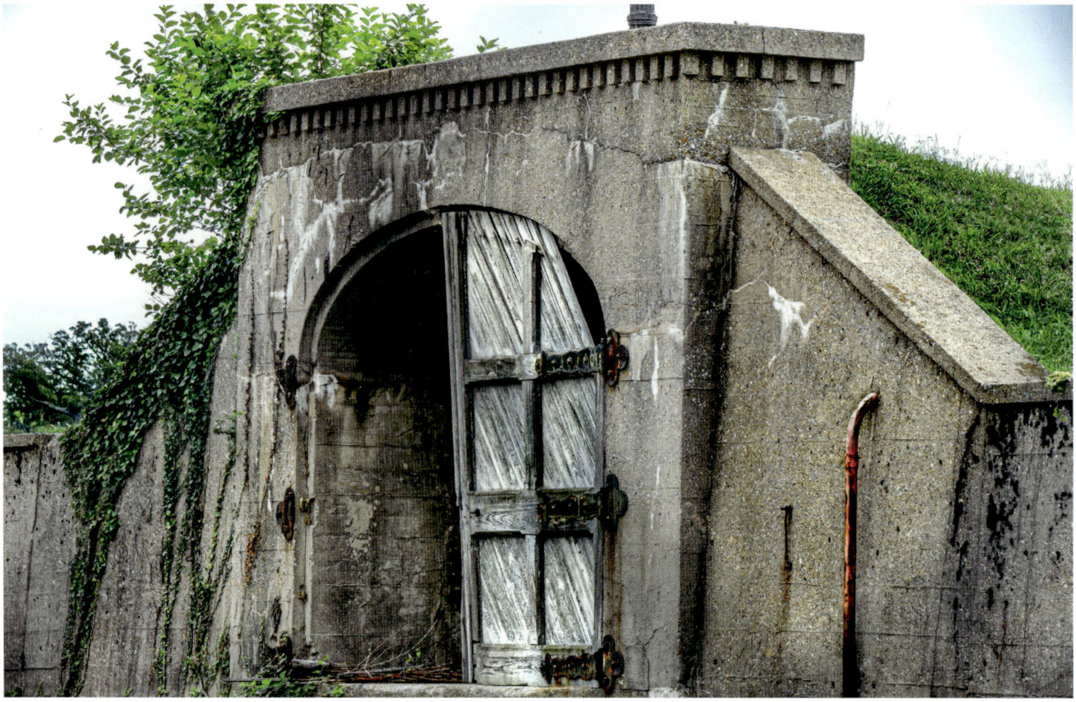

UNDERGROUND SAND CHAMBER ENTRANCE: D.C.'s typhoid epidemic prompted the need for a new city water filtration system.

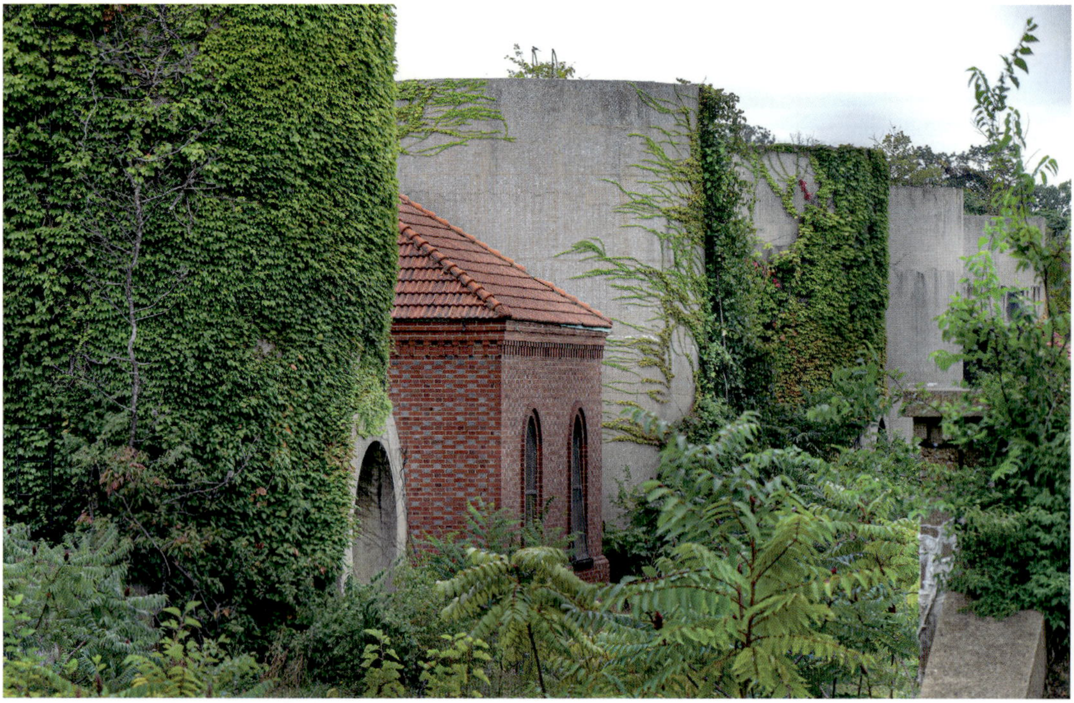

SAND SILO ROW: Raw water arrived from the reservoir and percolated through the sand in the twenty-five vaulted underground cells before flowing to D.C. taps. Sand was stored in silos.

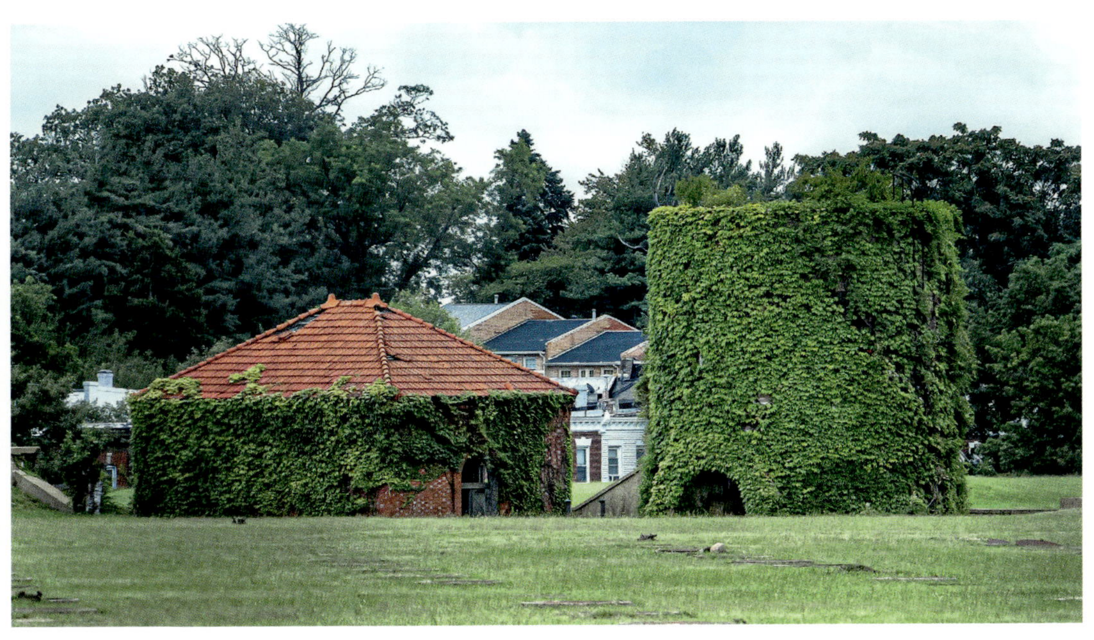

SAND SILO AND UTILITY BUILDING: The underground vaulted cells were lined with four feet of sand.

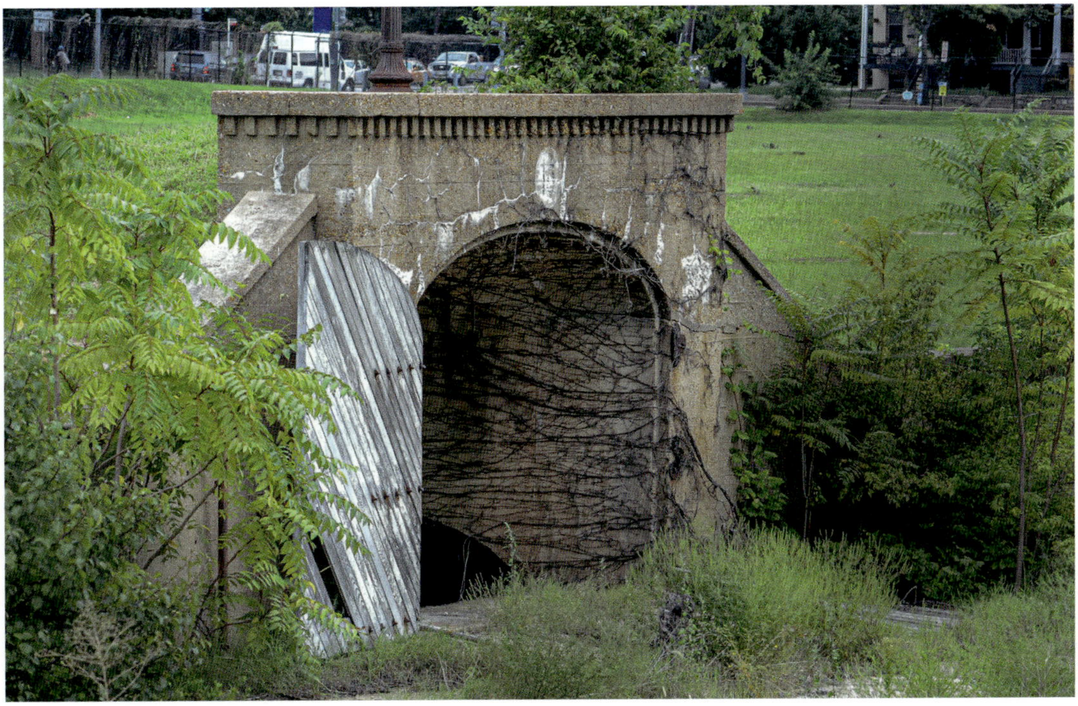

CATACOMB-LIKE SAND CHAMBER ENTRANCE: Sand arrived from Laurel, Maryland, via the B&O Railroad. Sand filled the chambers through 21,000 property manholes.

11

OLD SOLDIERS DO NOT FADE AWAY

The Soldiers' Home property is one of America's oldest veterans' retirement facilities, and embraces stunning buildings, bearing witness to history. Four of the original buildings are listed as national historic landmarks. Two of the buildings served as the summer White House for Presidents, including Chester Arthur, Rutherford B. Hayes, James Buchanan, and Abraham Lincoln. During the Civil War, Lincoln resided in what is now called Lincoln Cottage.

In 1851, a United States movement formed to fund a Soldiers' Home in Washington, D.C. A heroic General of the Mexican-American War, General Winfield Scott, received reparations in lieu of pillaging Mexico City. Accordingly, Scott paid his troops and forwarded the balance of the reparations to Congress along with a request to initiate a project to house the elderly and ailing soldiers; thus, the Soldiers' Home was born.

In its early days, the Soldiers' Home encompassed a 300-acre dairy farm for self-sufficiency, as well as the expectation that residents worked the farm for their room and board. During the twentieth century, though, the focus on resident life transformed from work toward an environment of rest, with the dairy farm evolving into a nine-hole golf course and gardens. Later, the complex admitted airmen and women and assumed a new marker, The Armed Forces Retirement Home ("AFRH").

Sixty-four buildings rest on the AFRH campus, with the inclusion of twenty-two vacant structures. The AFRH holds an impressive 272-acre footprint in Northwest D.C. The most architecturally stunning building, the Sherman Building, saw its abandonment for the first time in history only several years ago with the arrival of the 5.8-magnitude earthquake on August 23, 2011.

The Sherman Building suffered widespread damage with over 200 exterior masonry pieces detaching from the facade. Sherman's distinctive parapets were balancing precariously on their towers and faced imminent collapse in the aftermath of the earthquake. The 120-foot clocktower revealed large cracks, too. Emergency architectural stabilization measures for the Sherman Building were immediately set in motion because Hurricane Irene was on a path to pummel Washington, D.C. only four days post-earthquake. Fortunately, the round-the-clock architectural stabilization efforts prior to Irene's arrival were successful. Reconstruction and structural remediation thus commenced over the course of the next few years. The Sherman Building now houses AFRH's administrative offices, but when I visited it, Sherman was still vacant and in need of repair and renovation. The Sherman Building is a tough old soldier and stands as a stunning testament to history. Washington, D.C.'s tough old soldier, Sherman, while refusing to die, as in Gene Autry's song lyric, will not fade away either.

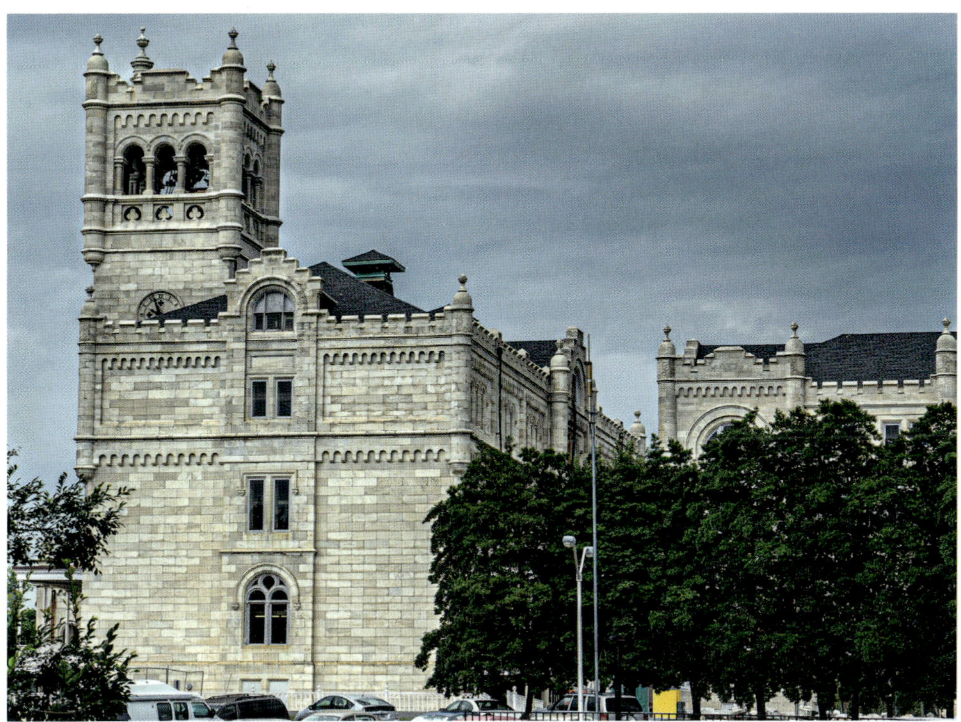

SHERMAN BUILDING: In 1851, the U.S. government purchased the Riggs estate, along with the neighboring property, to create a retirement home for registered soldiers.

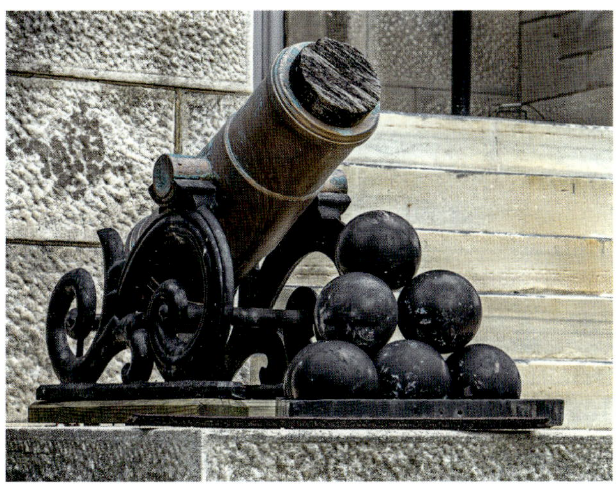

CIVIL WAR ERA RELICS: In its early days, the retirement home was self-sufficient and included a 300-acre dairy farm.

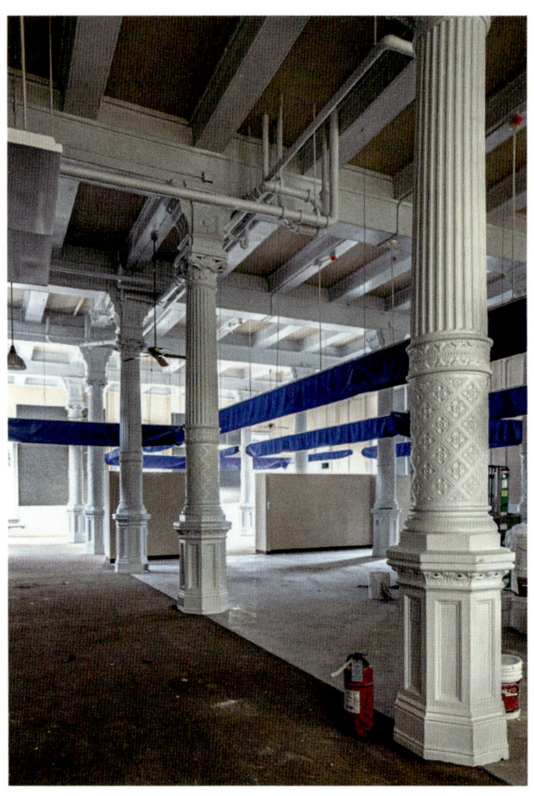

SHERMAN BUILDING INTERIOR RENOVATION: Since the retirement home's beginning, soldiers, and later airmen were responsible for site operational management.

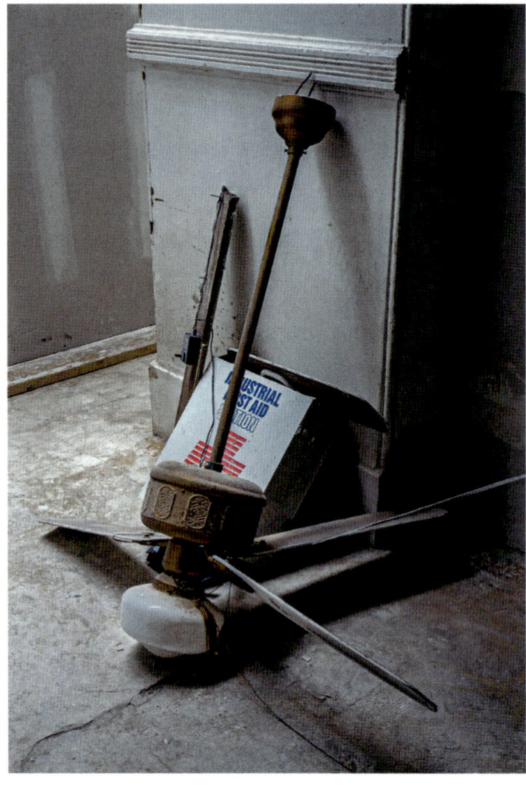

REPAIRS FOLLOWING EARTHQUAKE: In 2001, the U.S. Naval Home and the U.S. Soldiers' and Airmen's Home incurred a name change to the Armed Forces Retirement Home.

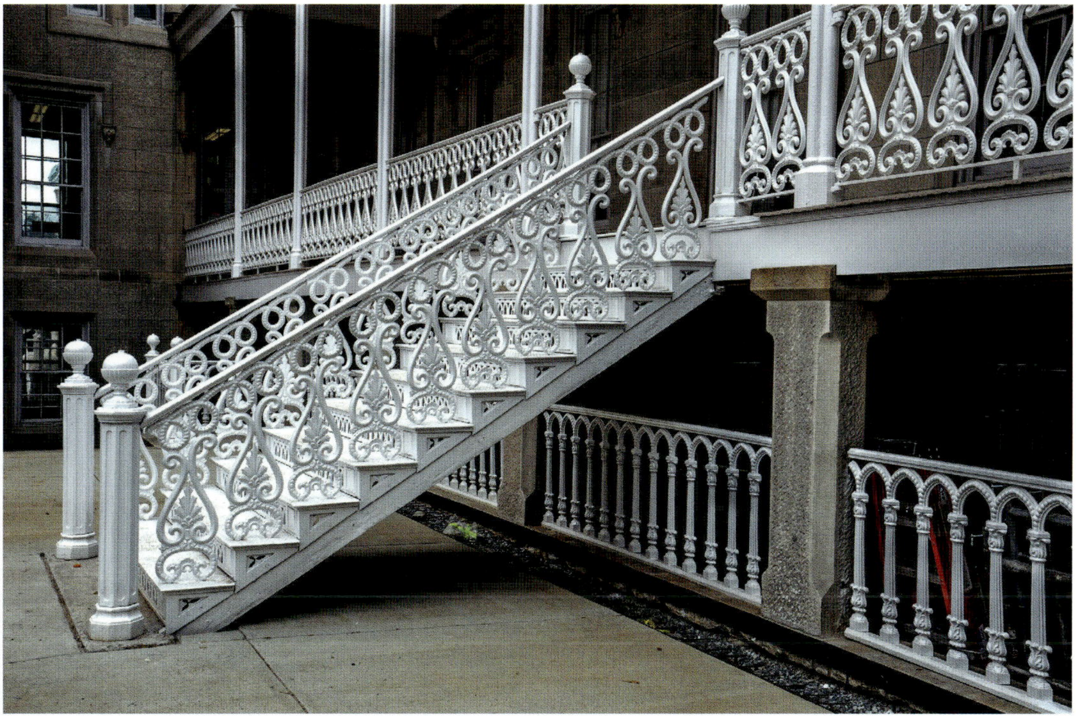

CAST IRON DETAIL ON SHERMAN BUILDING VERANDA: In 2007, the retirement complex listed as a historic district in the National Register of Historic Places.

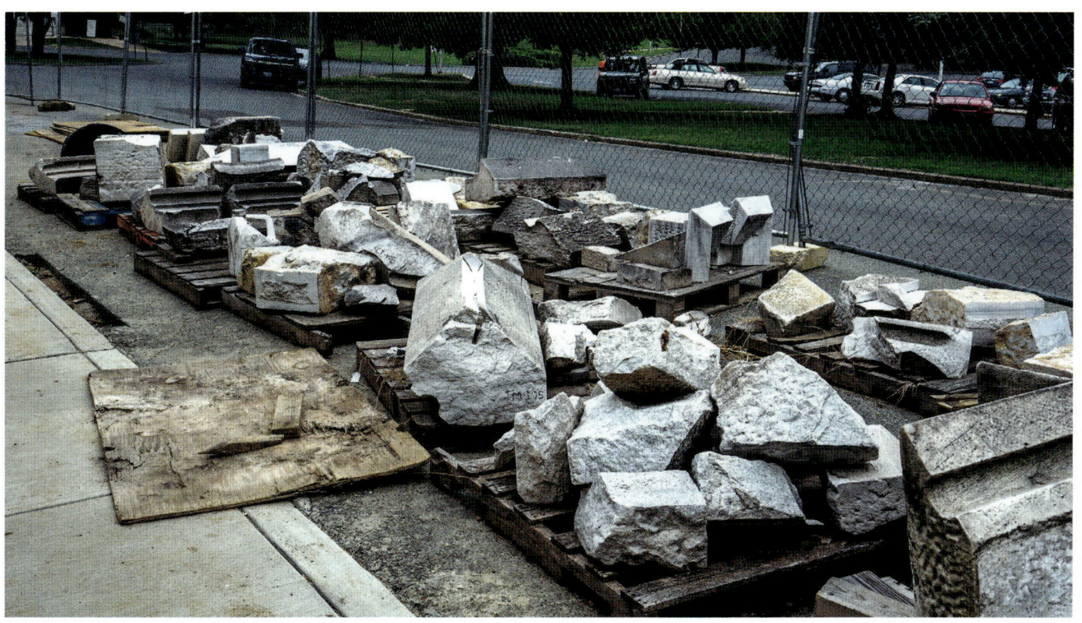

SHERMAN BUILDING MASONRY DISPLACEMENT FROM EARTHQUAKE: In the aftermath of 2011's 5.8-magnitude earthquake, 200 pieces of masonry fell from the Sherman Building. Emergency stabilization procedures were implemented immediately after the quake due to Hurricane Irene's arrival only four days later.

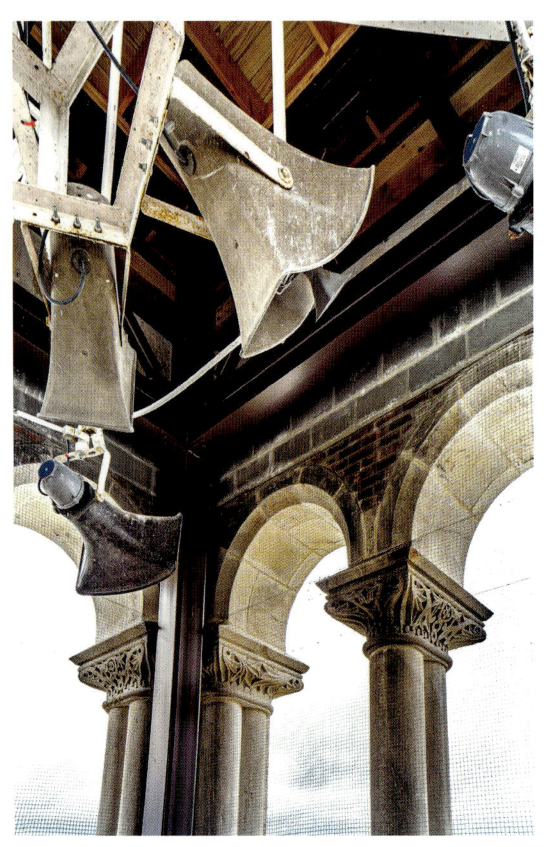

▲ **SHERMAN BUILDING BELL/CLOCK TOWER:** The bell/clock tower is 120 feet tall and sustained structural cracks from the 2011 earthquake.

▼ **LINCOLN COTTAGE FROM SHERMAN BUILDING BELL/CLOCK TOWER:** Lincoln Cottage was the first retirement home. President Lincoln resided in the cottage during the Civil War and during the summer. Lincoln's Emancipation Proclamation was scripted at this location.

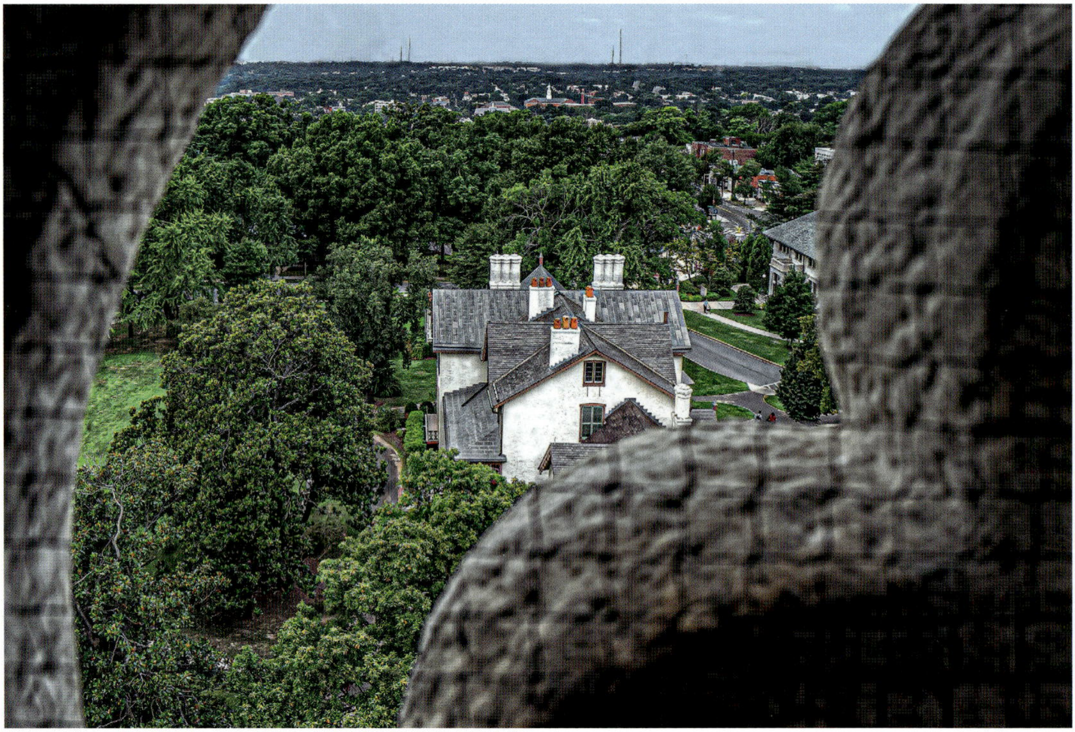

12

DO NOT ENTER

Washington, D.C. is a landscape of power and political symbolism, often revered, but equally criticized and subjected to crass sarcasm. I find it quite ironic that the Department of Homeland Security established its headquarters on a hilltop with a comprehensive view of D.C.'s dominion. The irony comes into play because, by virtue of its command, Homeland Security can project fear. Still, Homeland Security also selected a location that holds a past embedded in fear—a portion of the infamous St. Elizabeth Hospital ("St. E's"). Like all large psychiatric institutions of the nineteenth-twentieth centuries, St. E's is not an exception concerning a former aura of dread. Does anyone ever want to enter the doors of any large institutional psychiatric facility? Such phobia and anxiety about our large mental health complexes runs deep in our culture—watch the many movies with an asylum as its backdrop, and one never wants to enter such a place. Right or wrong, there is an unkind mystery about these places, and too often, horror stories of patient residency eventually emerge. Now, Homeland Security rests on St. E's former looming roost to assume the oversee of the realm in more ways than one.

St. E's, founded in the 1850s and at this time known as the Government Hospital for the Insane, has an illustrious past and claimed some famous inmates, such as John Hinckley, Jr., President Reagan's shooter, Ezra Pound, the modernist movement poet, and Richard Lawrence, the failed assassin of President Andrew Jackson. The large campus was shut down in the mid-1980s as a result of Reagan-era deregulation when a place that originated as a humane alternative to warehousing the mentally ill was seen as obsolete—deinstitutionalization became the new norm. Patients were released *en masse* in the 1980s, and for a while, many of patients wandered amid St. E's abandoned hospital facilities. It was not until 2009 that the National Capital Planning Commission approved a Master Plan for St. E's redevelopment, starting with the new site for the U.S. Coast Guard Headquarters, and a few years later, the establishment of the Department of Homeland Security Headquarters.

St. E's was the first federally funded mental hospital in the United States. Claiming more than 250 acres, St. E's early days of operation included a dairy and a farm. Along with so many other such facilities, St. E's grew from a national movement promoted by psychiatrist, Thomas Kirkbride, and social reformer Dorothea Dix. These two idealists believed that majestic, light-filled buildings within a natural environment would promote curative effects on those with mental disorders. In its infancy, St. E's was progressive for its time, as each patient had a private room with views of nature, and St. E's did not discriminate against racial lines. Still, because of imminent overcrowding and limitations on resources, African Americans did not always receive the same standard of care as other residents. By the time of the Civil War, St. E's neared capacity and tents appeared on the grounds for patient overflow. Many of the single rooms held two or three patients.

Patient numbers continued to increase during World War II, and by 1955, 7,500 patients per day received treatment. St. E's struggled with securing funding in the 1970s, and this, along with a national pushback against large mental institutions, forced St. E's to downsize all services. In 1987, St. E's East Campus was transferred to the District, and the hospital is still in operation but with treatment provided to only about 250 patients—a fraction of the number once treated on the sprawling site. In 2002, St. E's ceased operations on its West Campus with the Department of Homeland Security and U.S. Coast Guard, assuming occupancy within West Campus buildings. Except for the West Campus and a portion of St. E's East Campus, vacancy claims the balance of St. E buildings. Plans for further development of the campus, though, are in motion.

Invariably, mental health care management continues to be a challenge faced by governments—federal, state, and local. What is the best health care plan, and how much should the government subsidize? On a primal level, Americans fear confinement—something drummed into our psyche for more than two centuries—liberty and freedom are always at the forefront of our subconscious. How do we help the many unable to help themselves and are unable to enjoy the fruits of freedom and liberty? Rational or not, the "do not enter" ambiance still prevails within the mental health treatment arena. The deinstitutionalization movement of the 1980s was a proven disaster for those needing help, yet, institutionalization was also a disaster; a needed balance seems unattainable, with the "enter" sign still spurned and ever so distant.

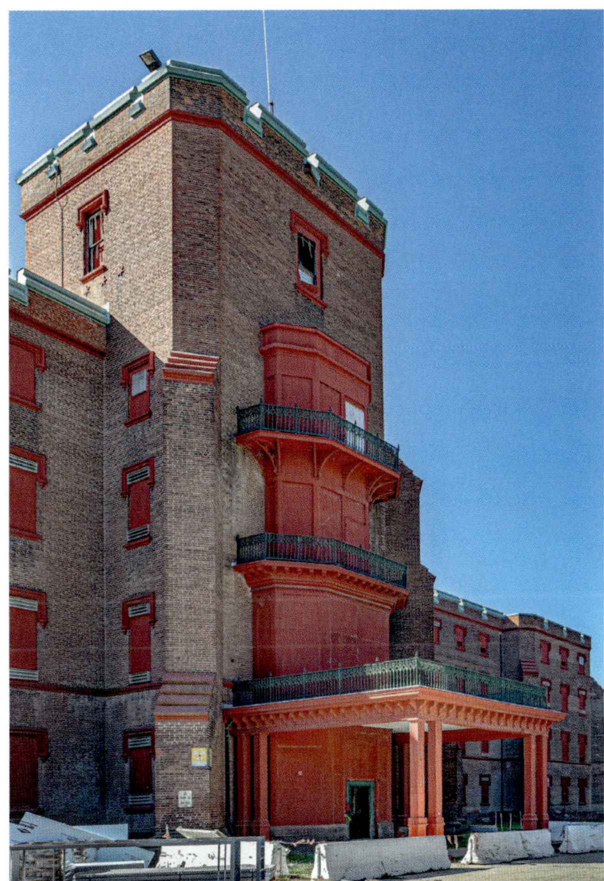

▲ **CENTER BUILDING:** Once a Kirkbride-designed hospital, St. Elizabeth's (St. E's) Center Building is undergoing renovation as the new headquarters of Homeland Security.

▼ **GREENHOUSE SECTOR:** A large greenhouse complex sits on St. E's 350-acre property.

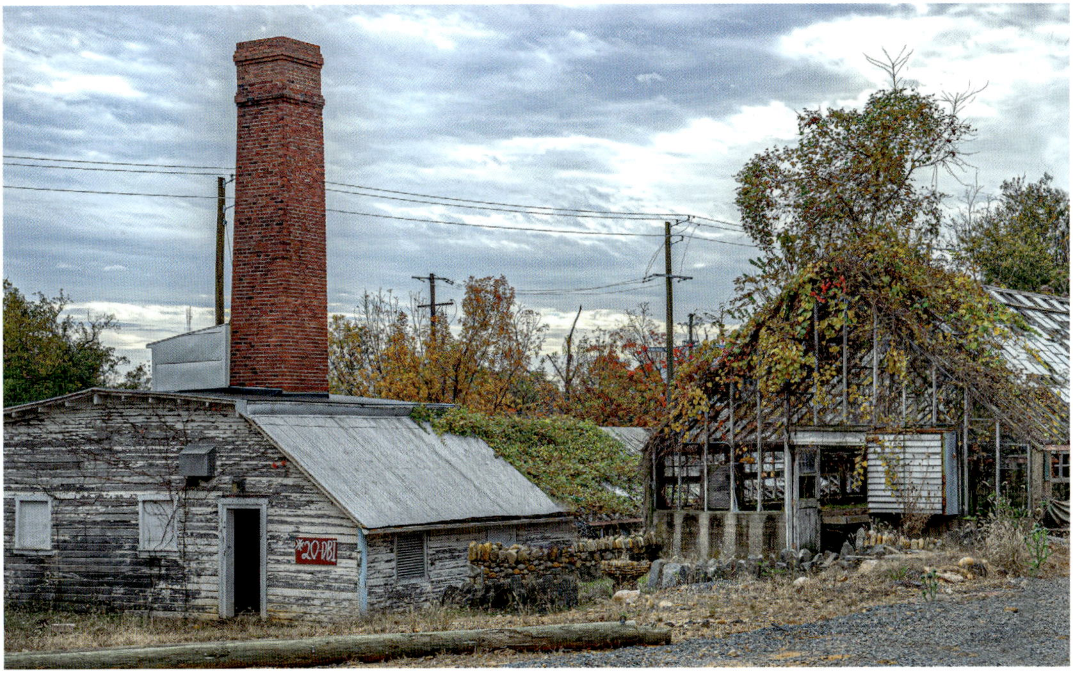

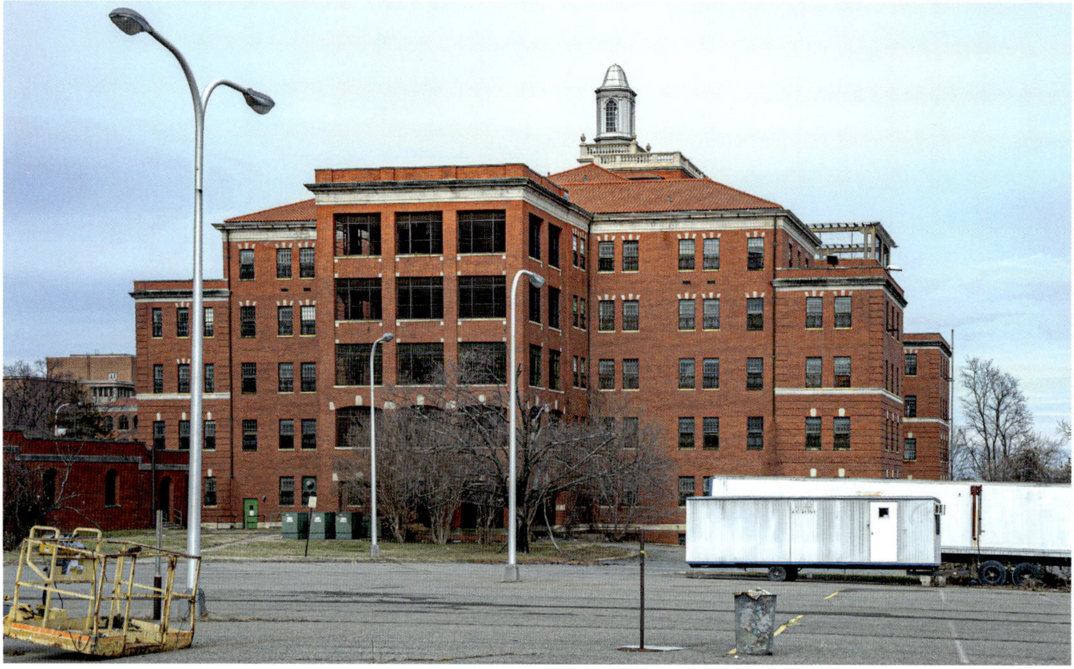

HOSPITAL: The 2009 Master Plan for the redevelopment of St. E's, preserves the historical flavor of the West campus and the incorporation of sustainable development.

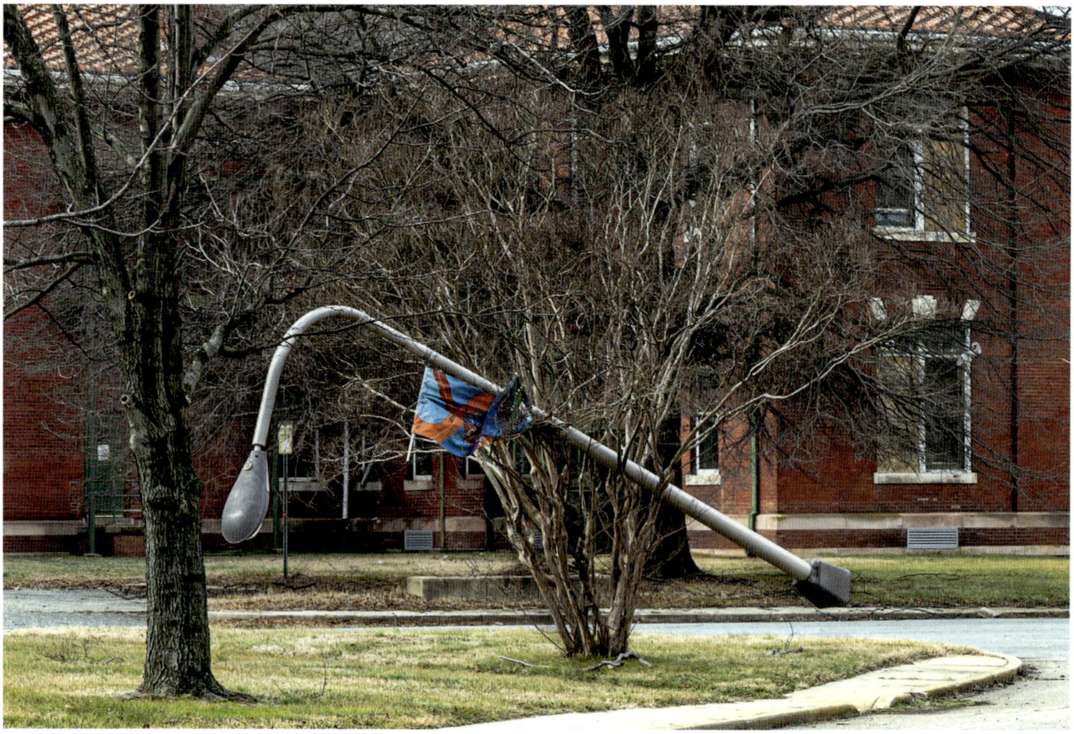

HOSPITAL: St. E's redevelopment Master Plan includes the preservation and repurposing of fifty-one of sixty-two buildings on the West Campus.

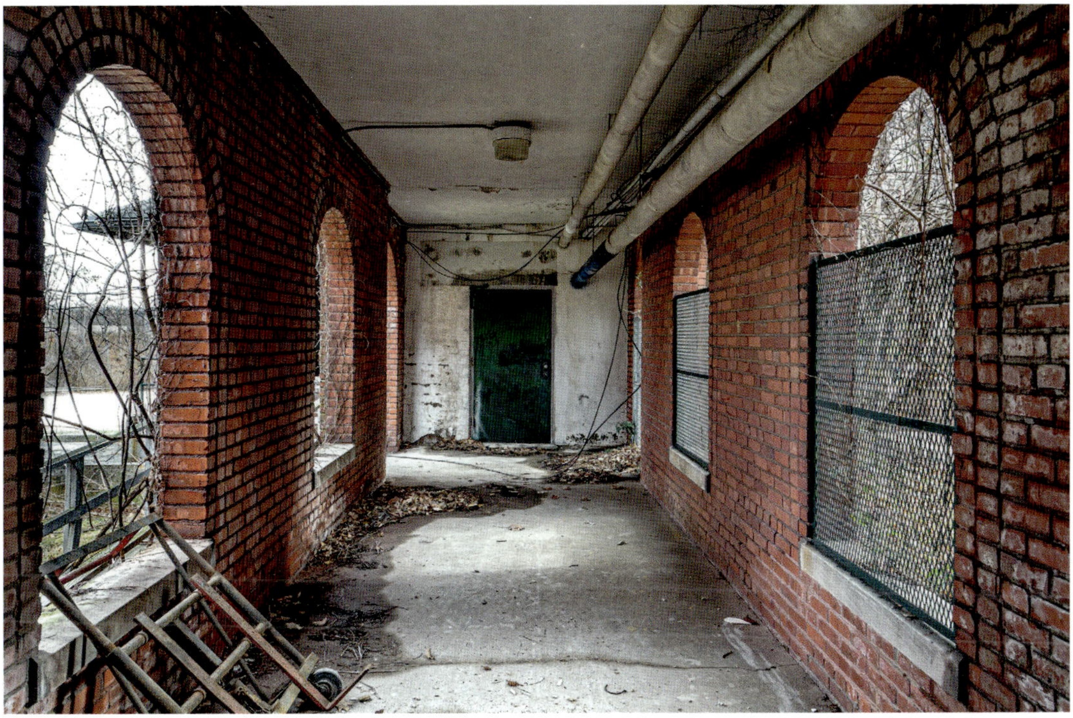

▲ **HOSPITAL CORRIDOR:** St. E's Master Plan includes considerations for offices, childcare centers, fitness centers, cafeterias, a credit union, a barbershop, conference facilities, library, and storage.

▼ **HOSPITAL CORRIDOR:** The last construction phase of St. E's Master Plan notes a new headquarters for the Federal Emergency Management Agency, the Transportation Security Administration, and Immigration and Customs Enforcement, Customs, and Border Protection.

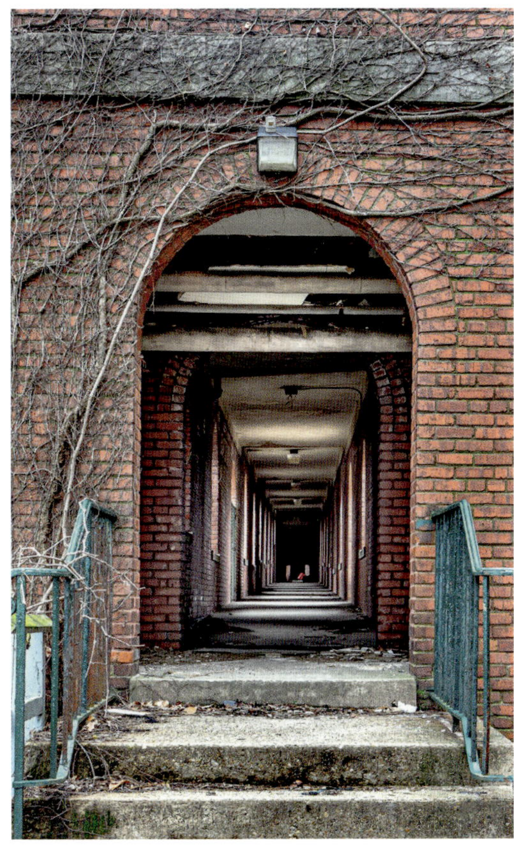

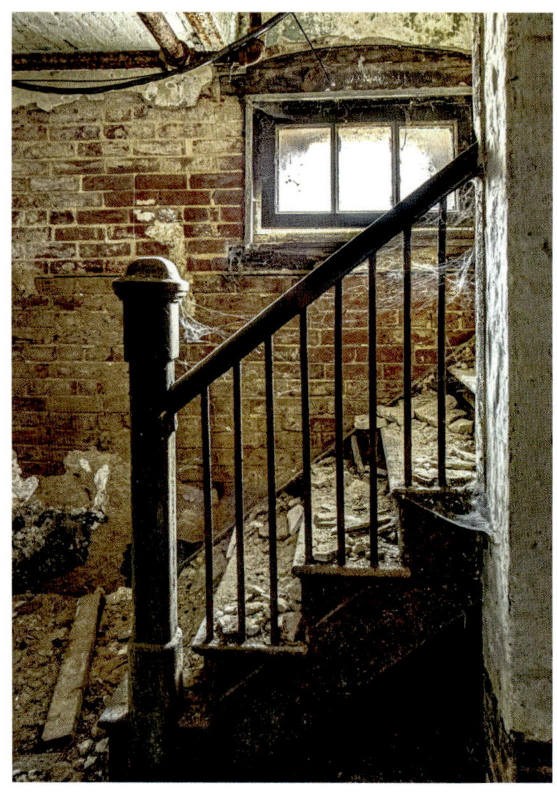

BASEMENT: In several phases of development, St. E's current Master Plan extends to the next five to twenty years.

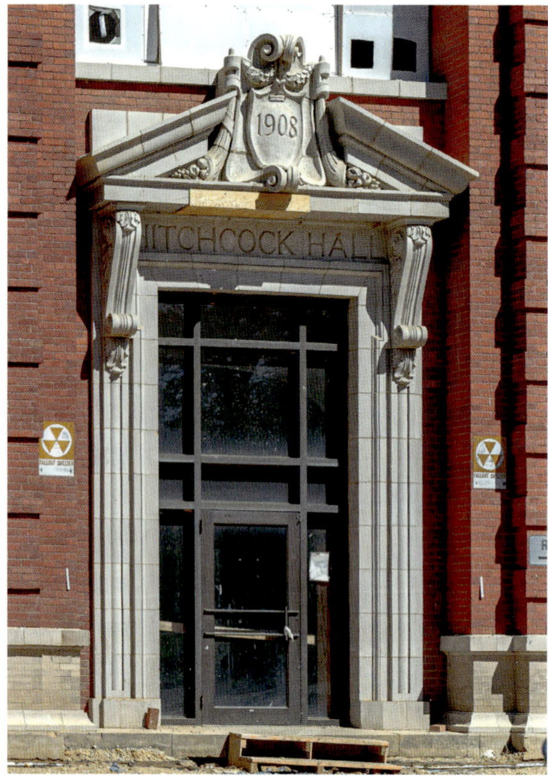

HITCHCOCK HALL: Built in 1910, Hitchcock Hall was a venue for patient entertainment.

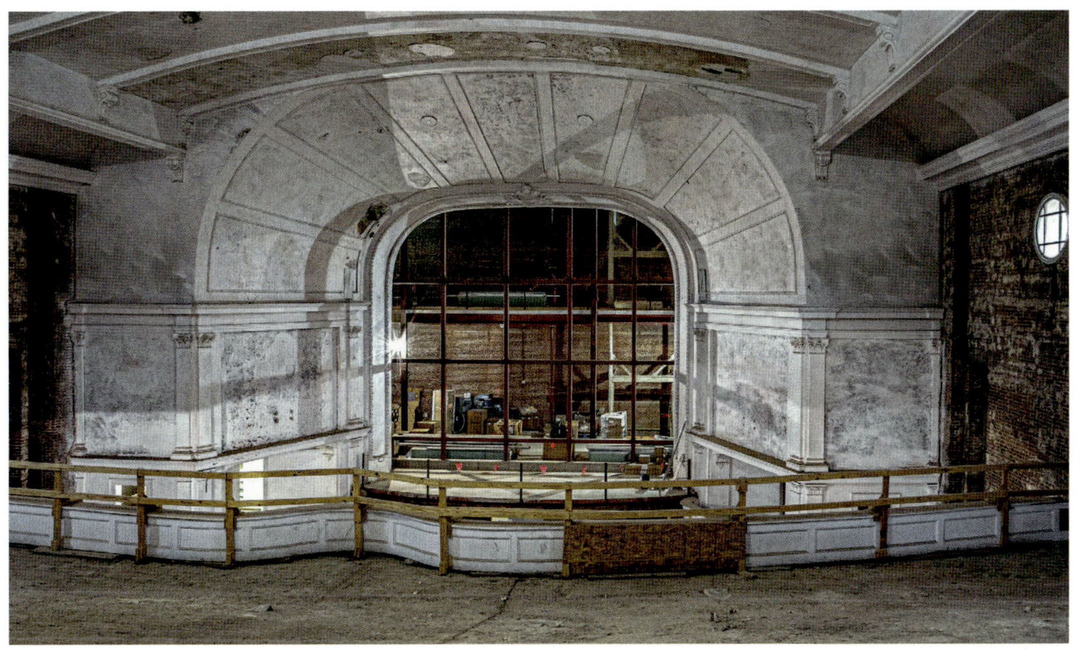

HITCHCOCK THEATER RENOVATION: Hitchcock's capacity is 1,200 and provided entertainment such as vaudeville, operas, musicals, dances, lectures, and movies.

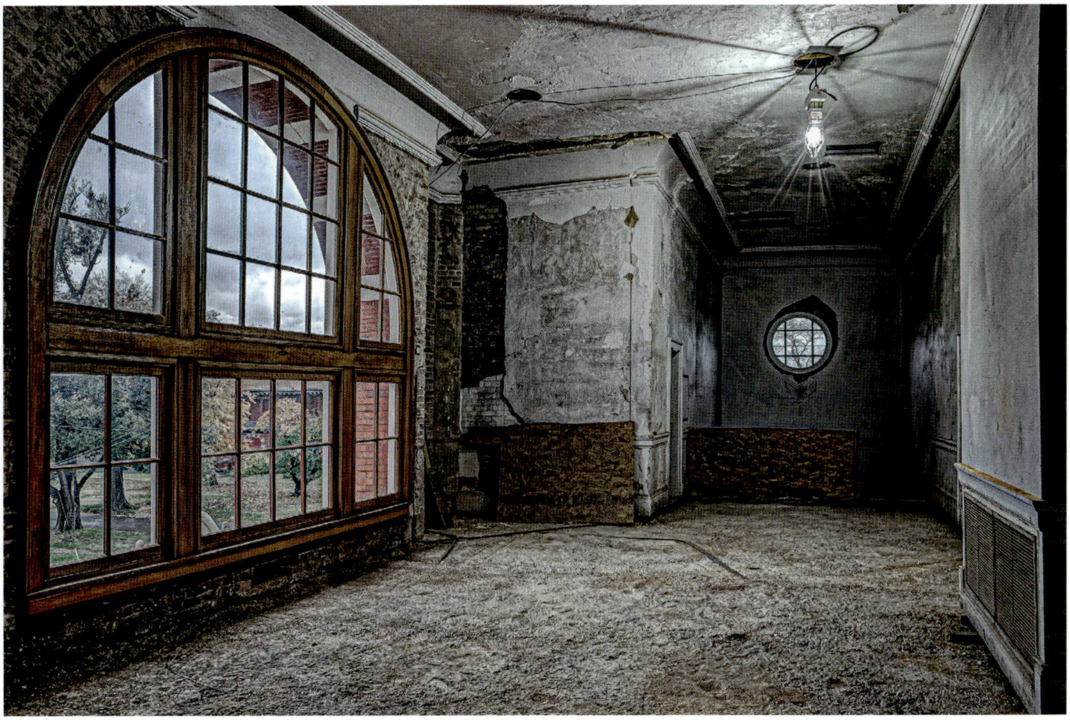

HITCHCOCK HALL LOBBY: A small chapel in Hitchcock's basement once served St. E patients.

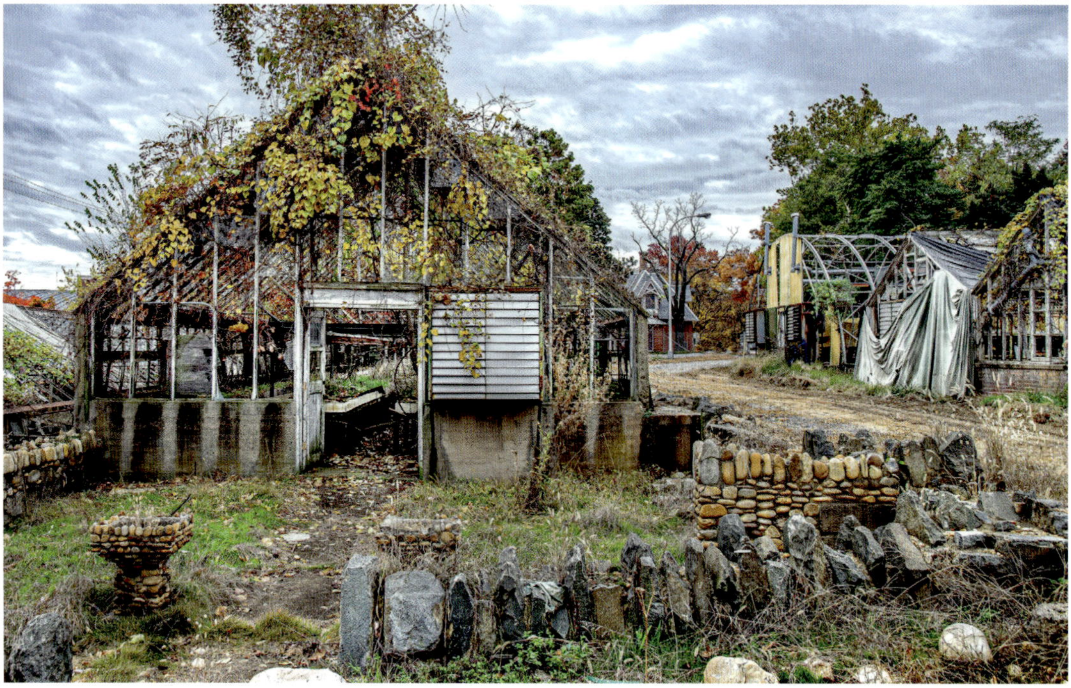

GREENHOUSE SECTOR: St. E's produced most of their food on site until the turn of the twentieth century. Patients often tended the farm fields.

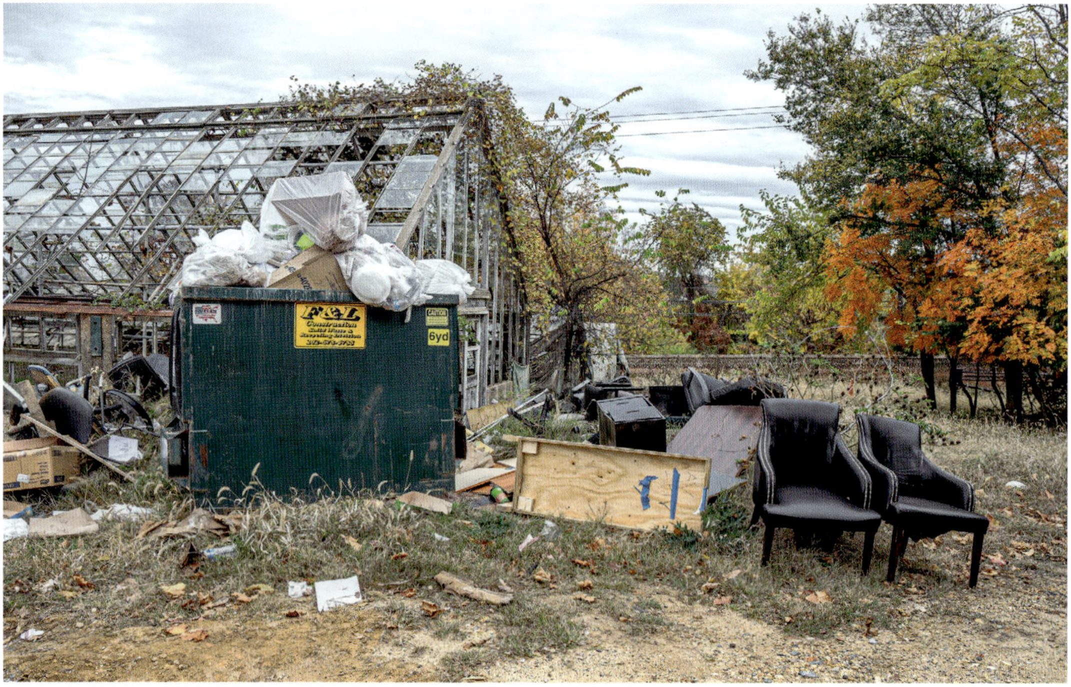

GREENHOUSE SECTOR: St. E's holds two cemeteries on its property. Graves include the burials of those from the Civil War, including Union and Confederate, as well as Native Americans, indigent, and friendless people. Some graves are unmarked.

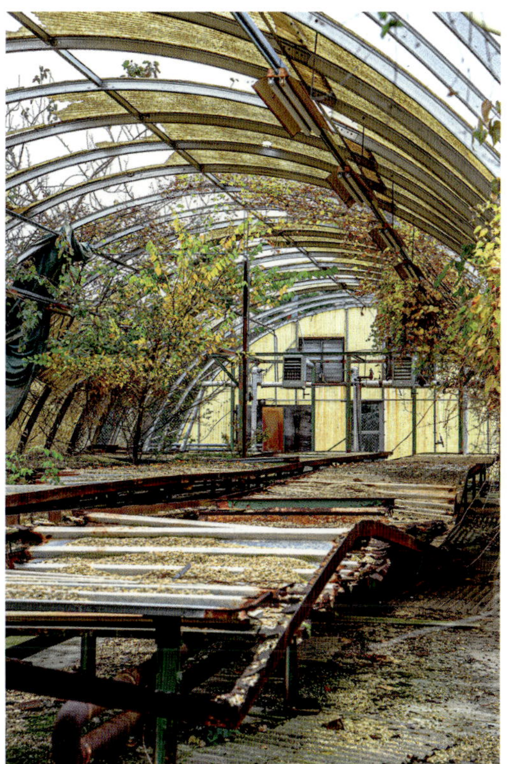

GREENHOUSE SECTOR: St. E's strived for self-sufficiency with food and energy and had a power plant.

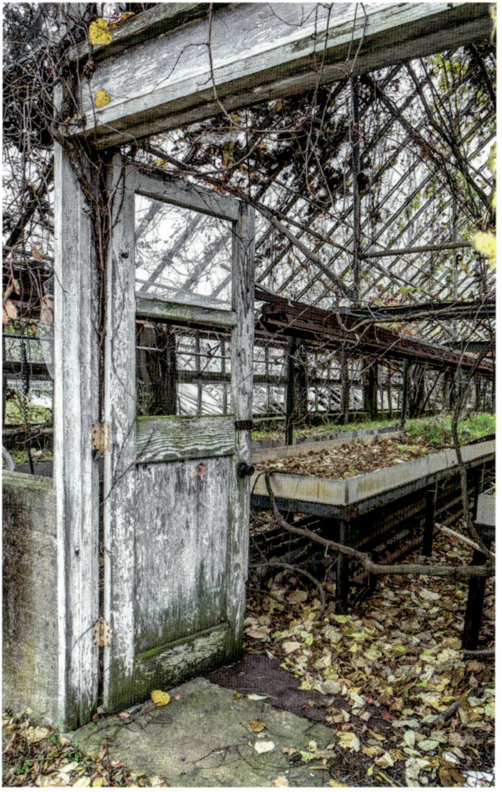

GREENHOUSE SECTOR: At one time, St. E's quartered horses and about 600 pigs. In addition to greenhouses, the property included a dairy and a canning operation.

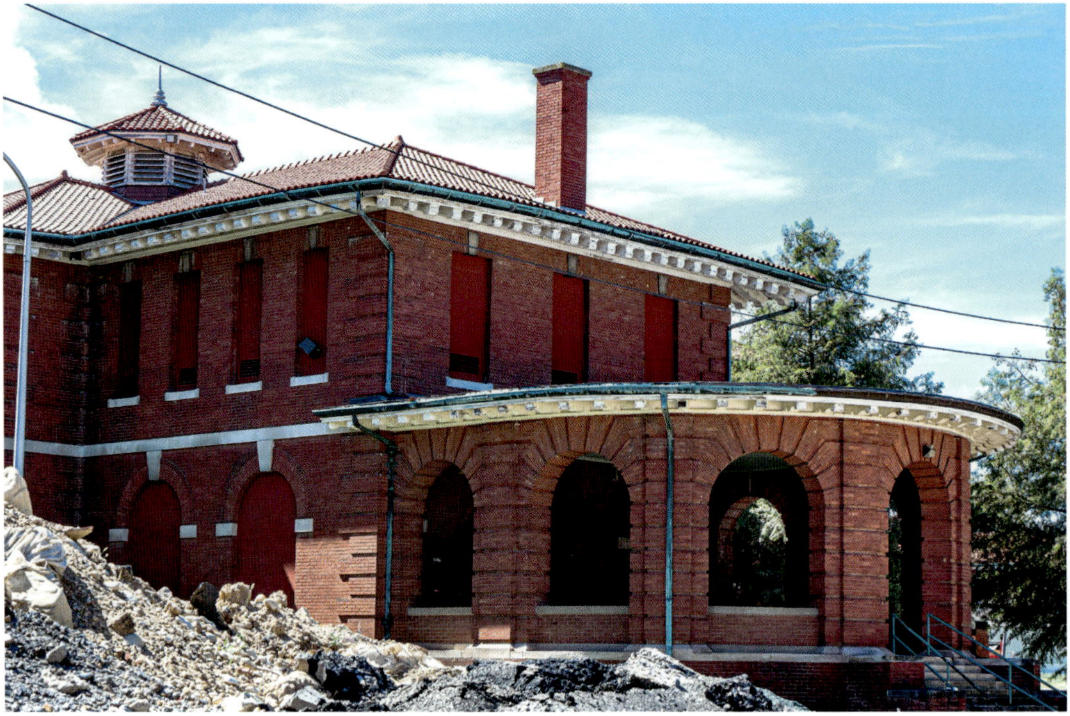

ST. E's WEST CAMPUS: Between 1850 and 1950, St. E's expanded as a treatment and research facility.

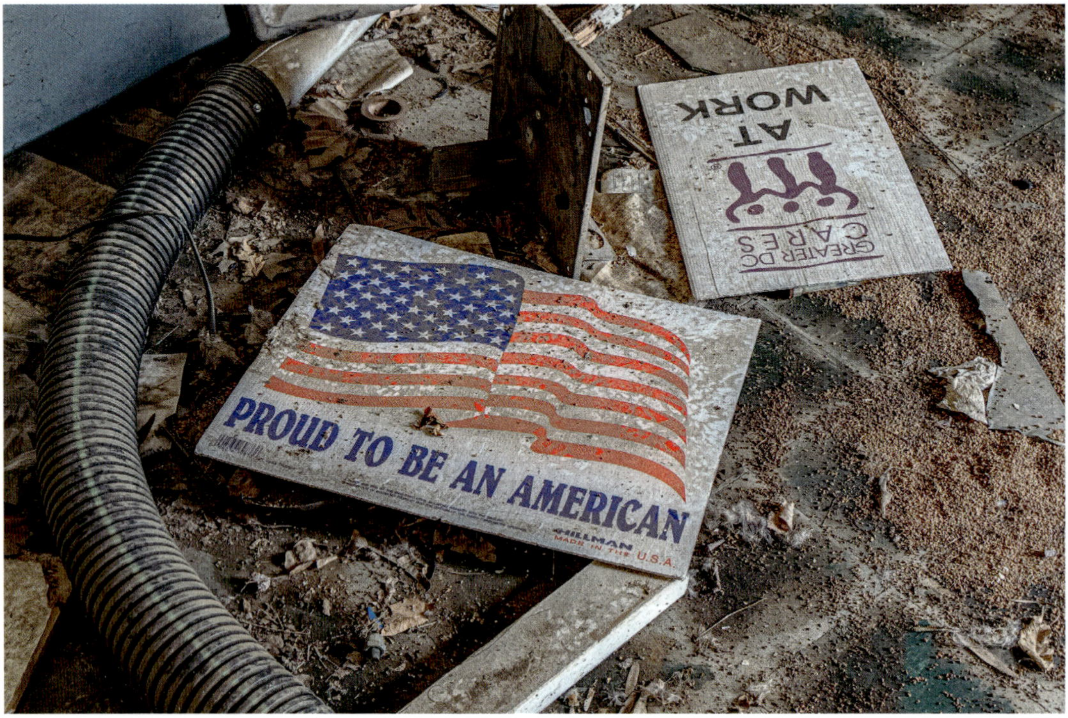

ARTIFACTS: Patients participated in various recreational activities, including boxing, croquet, baseball, dancing, horseshoes, puzzles, and reading.

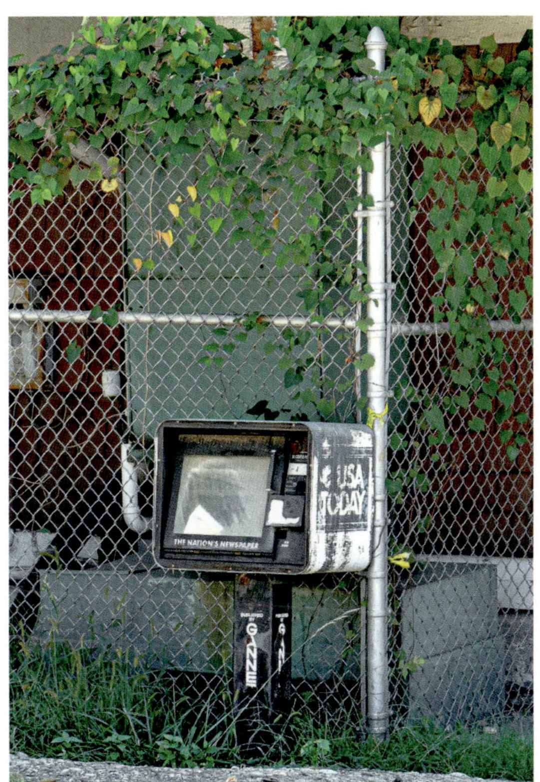

USA TODAY VENDING MACHINE: The twentieth century incorporated scientific methods for mental health treatment as technologies and therapies evolved.

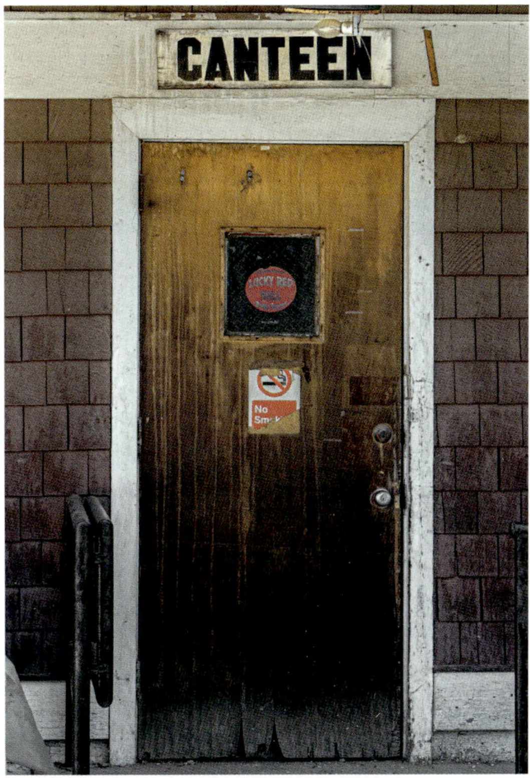

CANTEEN: St. E's was the first public mental health hospital to train medical interns.

13

THE WORDS OF THE PROPHETS

Graffiti and street art regularly join with controversy as this art is often presented on stone canvas as proclamations of protest or social change. In so many urban settings, and often within areas rife with derelict structures, graffiti is a common feature. Street art, graffiti's recognized sister, which is often authorized and endorsed, has a more revered place in communities, but frequently holds to bold outcast statements.

The beginnings of graffiti are loosely traced to prehistoric times by way of petroglyphs on rock walls or cave paintings as a means of communication. The art form of graffiti as a social statement is a broad concept, and the art itself takes many forms—from basic identification tags, to quickly scribbled expressions of dissent and politics, to elaborate and exquisite murals. Graffiti often highlights societal incongruities and has frequently been associated with civil unrest. While graffiti is, at times, a form of protest, street art, frequently, is sanitized for public acceptance with works often commissioned or created with consent. Some view street art as caving to the forces of gentrifications, but both graffiti and street art hold the commonality of an artist leaving his or her mark on the physical environment. Because graffiti and street art are often temporary with removal a possibility at any moment, the transitory nature of this art demands abrupt notice and therefore is audacious, by virtue of its sense of immediacy.

Urban neighborhoods hold a richness of culture and experience given so many powerful and not always pleasant memories associated with their public spaces. Graffiti and street art offer great contributions to cultural heritage. This art form is the voice of the public, speaking out in an often clever and succinct manner, on political, social, or economic issues. Could this voice be akin to the instance of a prophecy "written on a wall" in the Old Testament Book of Daniel? The Book of Daniel presents a warning, in this case, about the imminent fall of a king. It is from this source we draw the common English expression "the writing's on the wall" as a premonition of doom. A modern variant, such as the lyric in Simon and Garfunkel's classic song, Sounds of Silence, "the words of the prophets are written on the subway walls and tenement halls," is a warning to pay heed to the prescient modern-day bards. In other words, the artists and thinkers hold the real answers to life and teach us a great deal about the world we live in. Go forth and read the walls of your towns and cities.

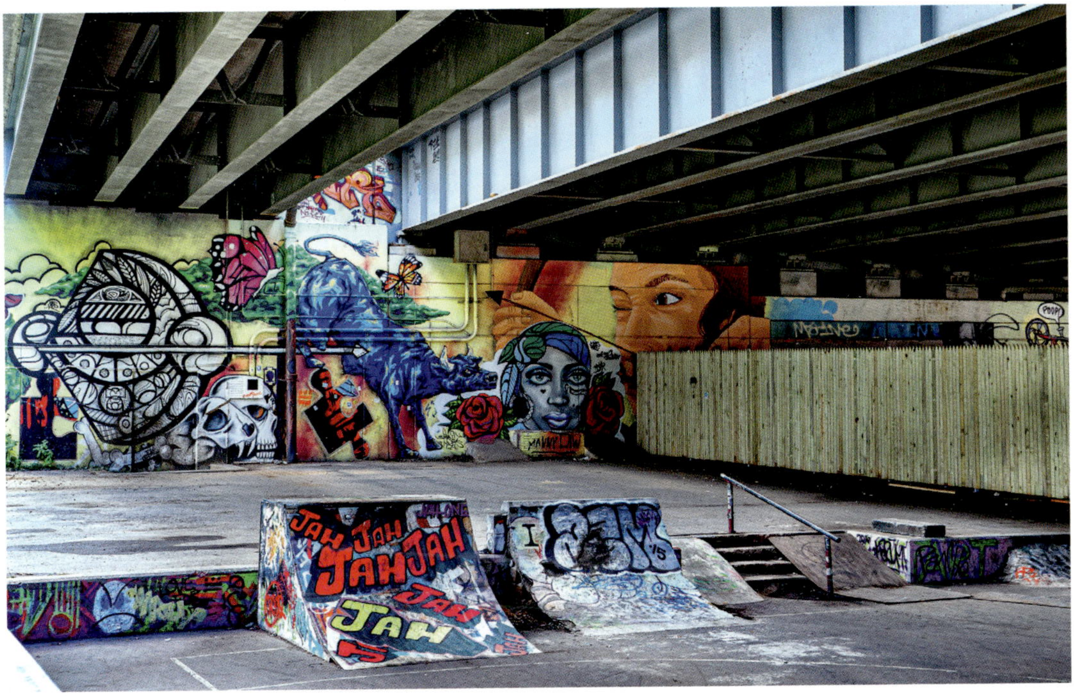

BELOW THE SOUTHEAST FREEWAY: The cement pad beneath one of D.C.s busiest highways is a canvas for graffiti artists and an improvised skateboard park.

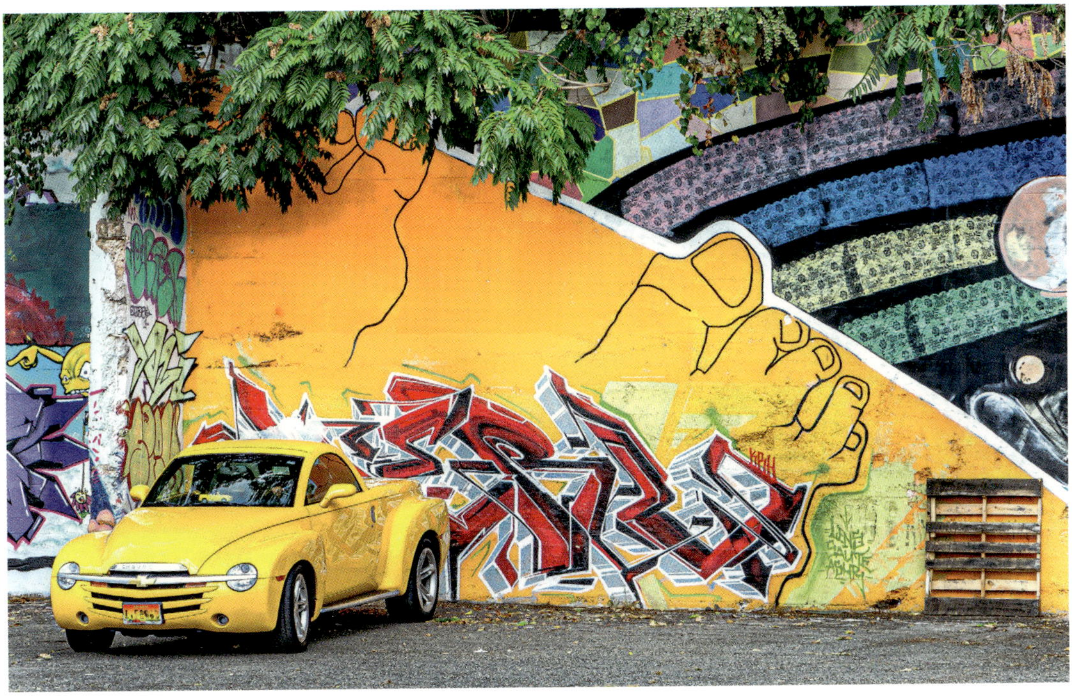

RHODE AVENUE RETRO MURALS: The yellow car seems like a coordinating accessory to one of the street murals featured in the "From Edgewood to the End of the World" art project.

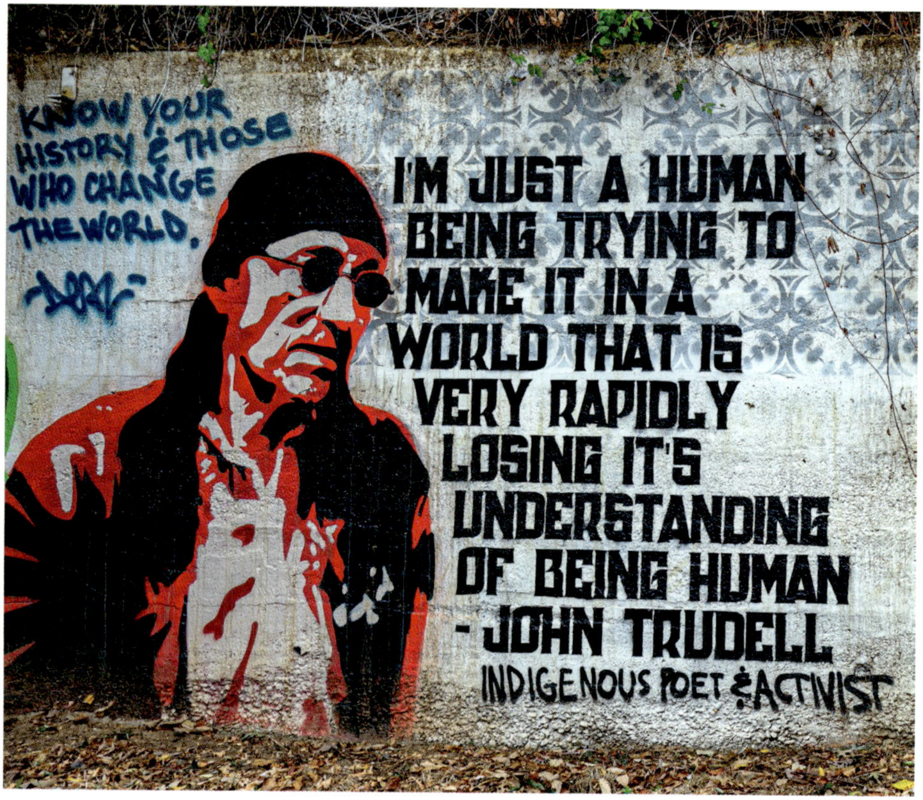

"FROM EDGEWOOD TO THE EDGE OF THE WORLD" PROJECT: Five artists, including forty young apprentice street artists contributed to the D.C. Commission on the Arts and Humanities art project.

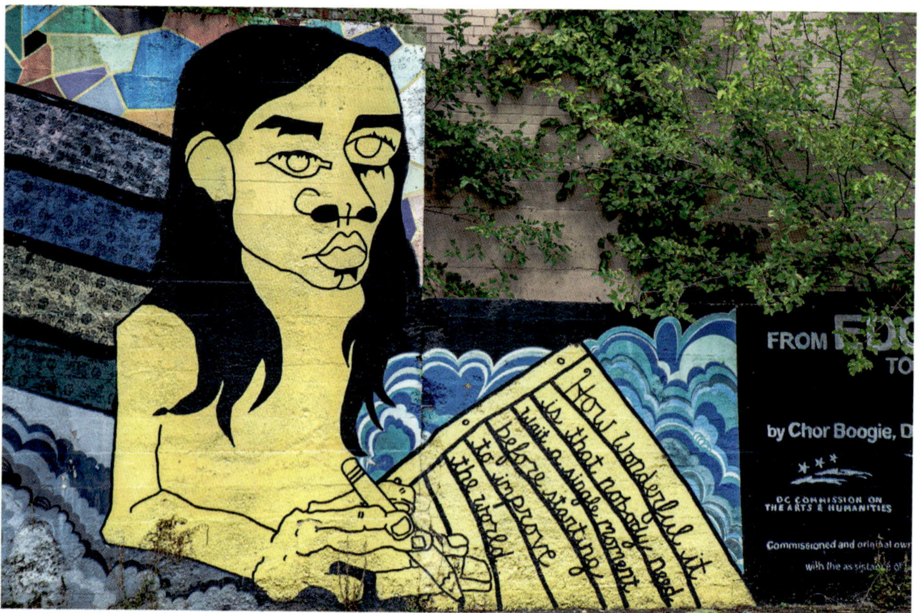

ALBERT CAVUS'S OPEN WALLS PROGRAM: Street artists created art along a 700-foot retaining wall visible from the Rhode Island Avenue Metro Station in D.C.

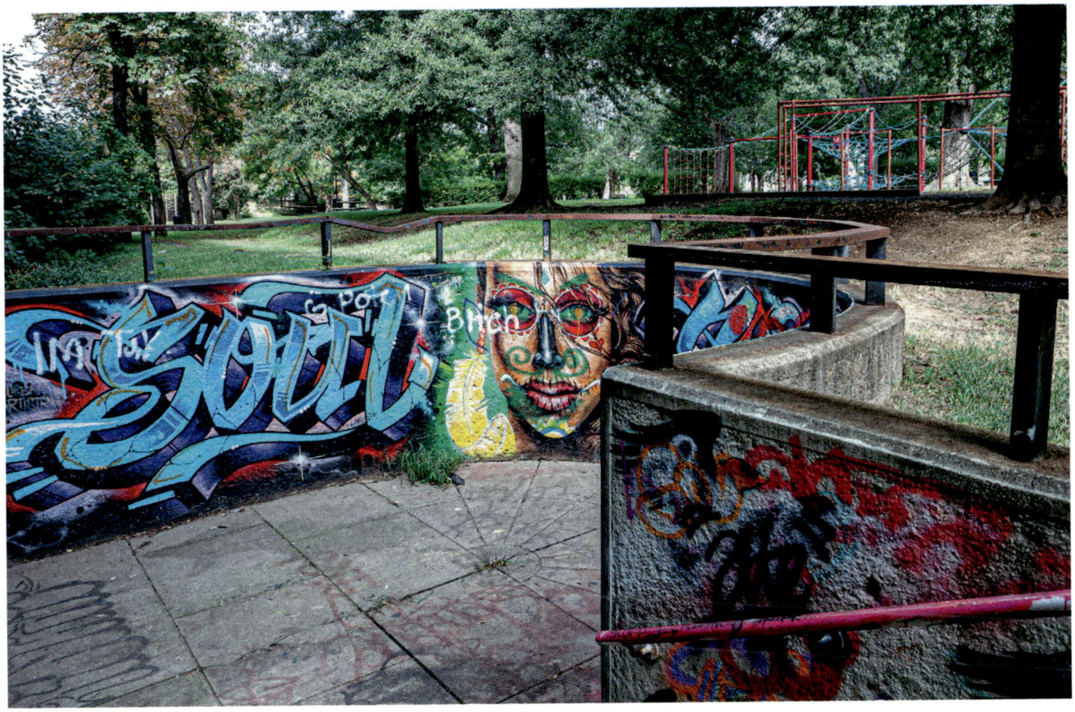

OPEN EXPRESSION NEAR THE CAPITOL SOUTH METRO STATION: The greens and jungle gyms of Garfield Park are the backdrop for graffiti artists.

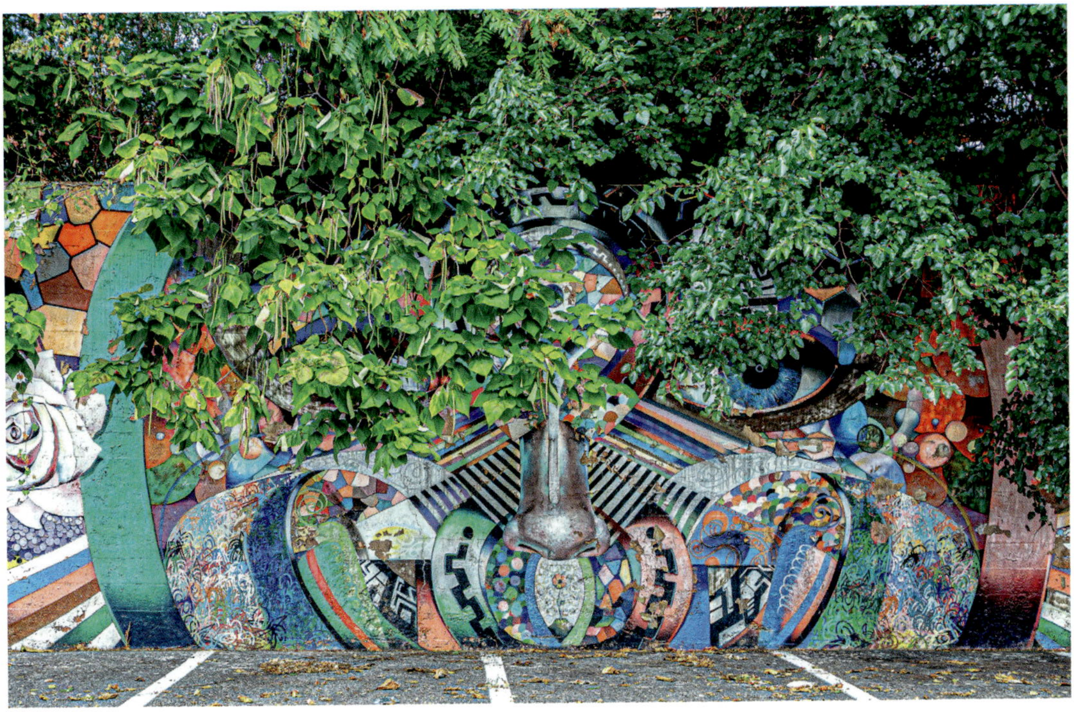

RHODE AVENUE RETRO MURALS: Albert Cavus's Open Walls Program is an artist collective allowing artists to create their artful expressions.

14

SCRAPS

This chapter is a small homage to the few abandoned sites and artifacts found within the boundaries of Washington, D.C.—those that did not fit into neat, compartmentalized chapters. These cast-offs are worthy of a look and, and like all abandonments, deserve recognition and meaning for their forsaken statuses. If anything, these images, like almost all abandoned exemplifications, are at the base, symbolic of our wasteful society. These scraps also remind us of our historical roots, and whether they pull at the nostalgic heartstrings from a simple, joyful time, or are blunt symbols of disenchantment with an institution, technology or time, these scenes are profound statements of larger more unsettling representations of forfeiture.

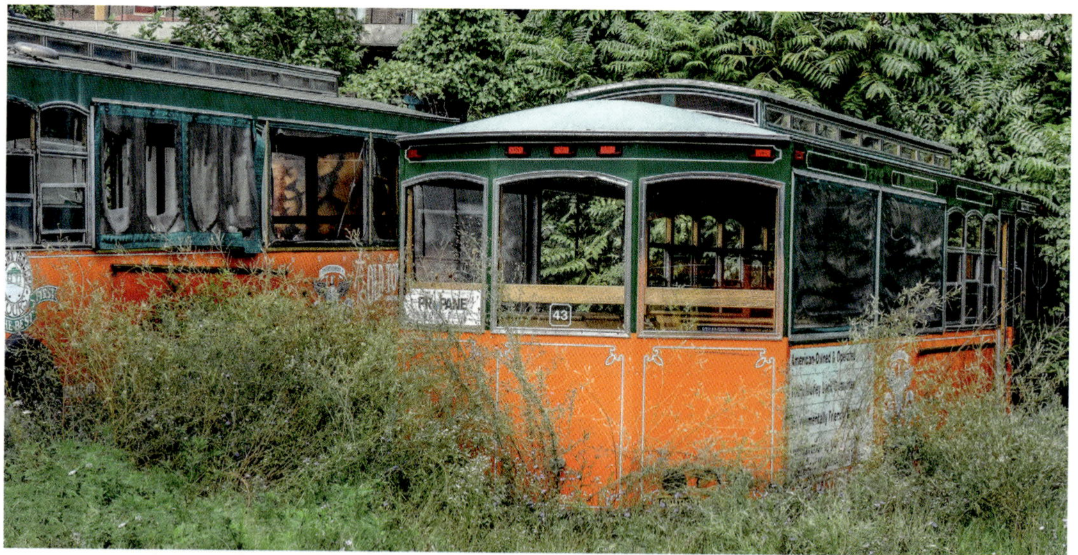

TOURIST TROLLEY CAR: Trolley Cars, such as this abandoned car, provide tours of Washington, D.C. sites.

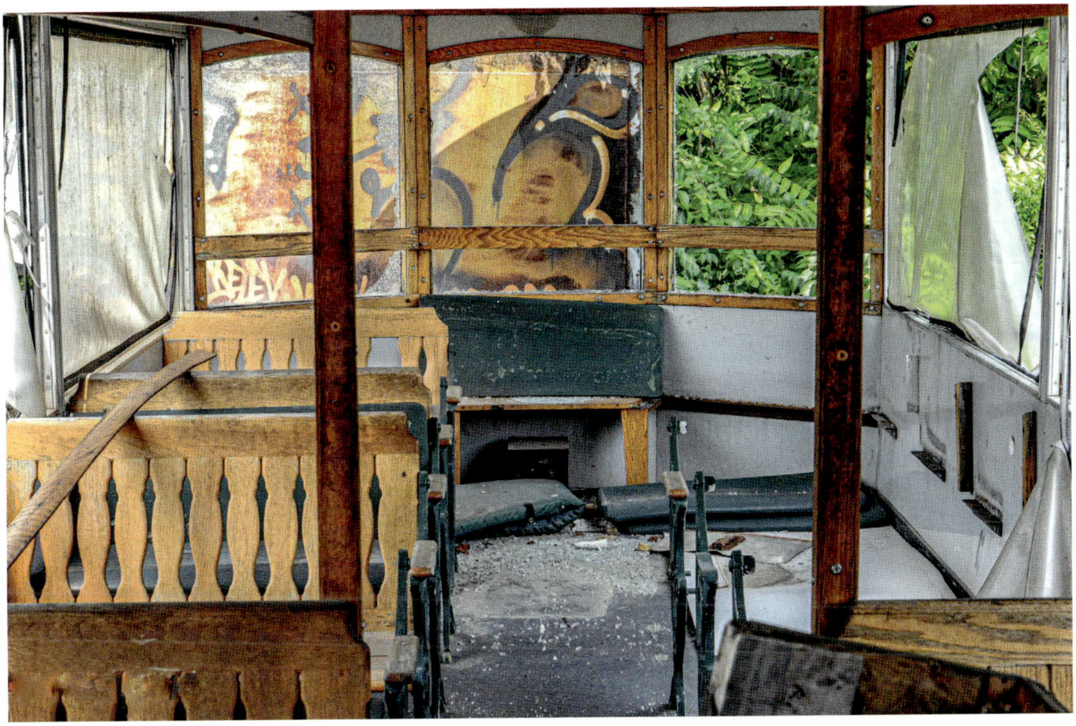

▲ **TOURIST TROLLEY CAR INTERIOR:**
For more than three decades, Old Town Trolley Tours served D.C.'s tourist trade.

▼ **CARDBOARD FAN IN TROLLEY:**
Tourists often need some assistance with adjustment to D.C.'s summer heat and humidity and were given cardboard fans during tours around the city.

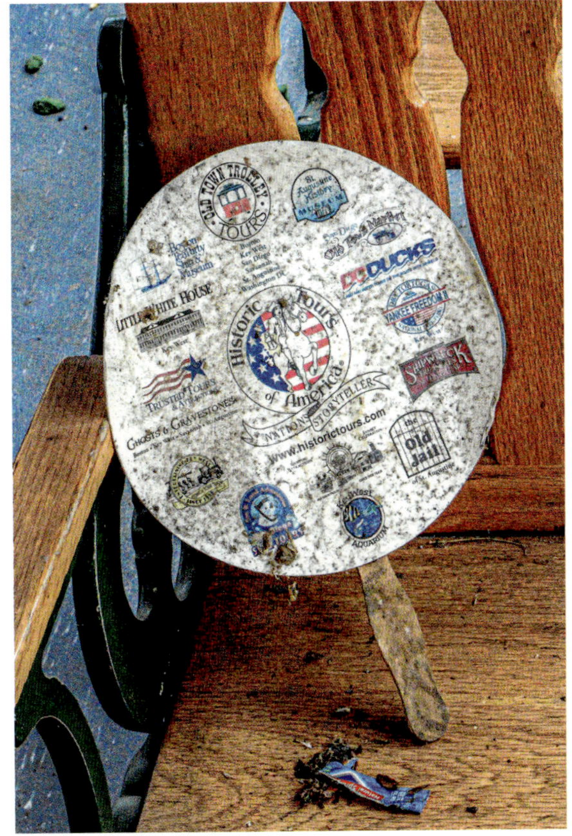

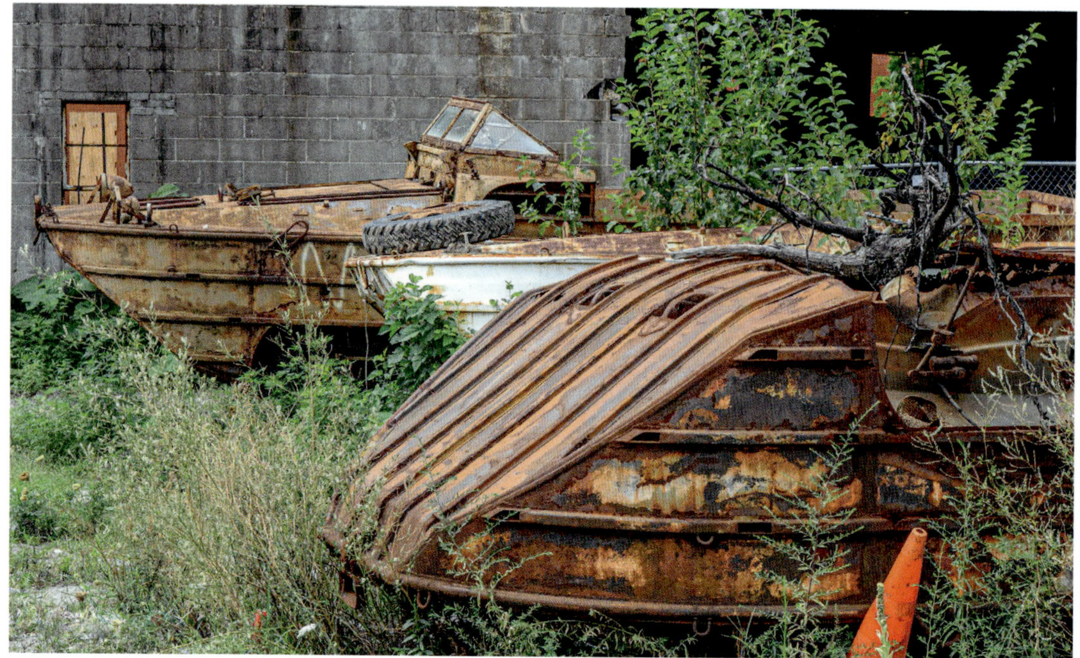

DUCK BOAT: World War II Era Duck Boats serve tourism along the Potomac River and provide unique glimpses of D.C. attractions.

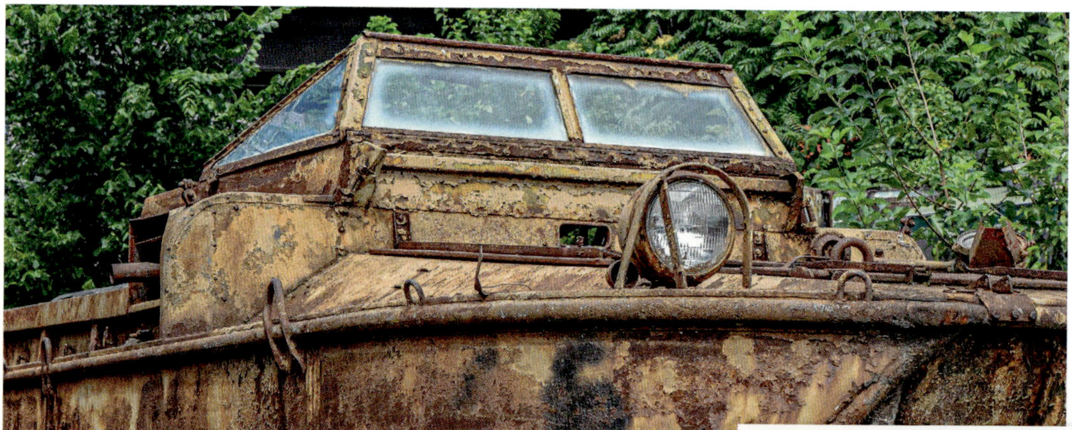

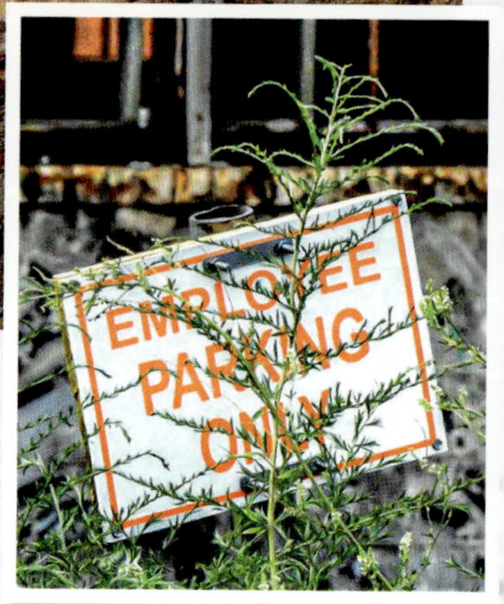

◄ **DUCK BOAT:** D.C.'s duck boat service has been cruising the Potomac since the 1990s, but the boats date to World War II.

► **RESTRICTED PARKING:** Weeds claim a parking spot reserved for a past employee at a once-thriving industrial facility.

15

SILENCE IS NOT GOLDEN

How does our mind's eye view the world without us? The images of vacant spaces, once dynamic, capture a departure from our everyday norms and instead present an alternate reality absent our presence. Is this one of the reasons I find urban exploration photography so captivating? Urbex environments are like alternate realities emptied of human life. Urbex imagery exposes how swiftly we can become estranged from our everyday lives, how our surroundings can suddenly become something fragile and tenuous. The urban explorer uses the camera to show where we once were, but no longer are.

Just like my urbex photo representations, the COVID-19 pandemic drives abandonment to a new alternate reality level. Images of evacuated streets and institutions make our common spaces unfamiliar. While life quarantined indoors, I captured some of the external environment emptied of life. As I shot the silent streets, I often felt alone in a desolate haunted space—and unlike abandonments, the setting was neat and tidy—unnatural to my urbex eye.

So many images of city life assume that hordes of people are always present. In the time of COVID, such scenes expose only a few lonely figures, if any. The bigger picture, though, is that the fear of the pandemic has fostered a new fundamental fear—the fear of each other. These photographs expose how swiftly we can become estranged from our everyday lives and how our surroundings can suddenly become something unstable. Images of empty public spaces, similar to photos of abandoned sites deserted for decades, reveal the myth that we are indispensable to such space existence. Instead, we live in heartbreaking silence. When will things return to normal? Will they ever return to normal? Dramatic reality reshapes our mindsets and forces us to absorb and internalize everything as we solo-walk through our new alternate reality.

What day is it? Since the lockdown began, every day feels like a Sunday because we do not hear the sounds of weekday rush-hour traffic, nor do we hear the sounds of arena sporting events or pub crawls. We live in tragic stillness. To me, each day now feels like an urban exploration Sunday—wake up early, venture into the wilderness, and grasp the essence of abandonment and silence. I expect this type of abandonment and silence, but when an ordinarily hyper-active city abruptly is forced into a silent pause, our brain is oversensitive to such modification. In this case, silence is not merely a lack of commotion; it joins with the fear of human contact, along with fear's cousin, suspicion.

Just as we attempted to acclimatize to our novel heartbreaking muted world, however, another shock, in tandem, greeted our new sphere—the death of George Floyd. Instantaneously, our pandemic fears were momentarily pushed aside for a new crisis that brought forth protests coast to coast. Just a week prior to this event, Americans were isolating themselves, but suddenly, fears were kicked to the curb to present a voice to the world. These dynamic actions, though, demonstrate another type of abandonment: abandonment of needed institutional parameters. The contemporary protests must be viewed in the context of an institutional void. These protests are the organically driven mass shout of people anguishing under a system that no longer works for many. The system seems to be hindering personal stakes rather than helping. Are we facing the ultimate abandonment of democracy as well? Public trust is at stake. The erosion of democratic protections such as the eyes of the free press, the impartiality of the law, and the transparency of governing actions, moved the needle of public trust into negative territory. The protesters are railing against a fragmented system that is unable to respond to all that troubles America. Such a hollowed system might collapse in short order with the next straw on the camel's back.

I am writing this chapter at the height of the COVID pandemic and amid the nationwide protests. A national election arrives in four months. An election will not destroy all adverse effects of the pandemic, eradicate all racism, reinstate social bonds to full, or restore democracy to all of our Founders' principles. Still, an election might present a chance for a new mandate of reform and deliver a new magic wand of trust for repair. If skepticism continues to permeate our system, our country's regime will collapse, and democracy will enter the door of abandonment. The future of democracy hangs in the balance. I hope that after this book is released, after the November 3, 2020, election, I will not have an opportunity to create a book about abandoned democracy.

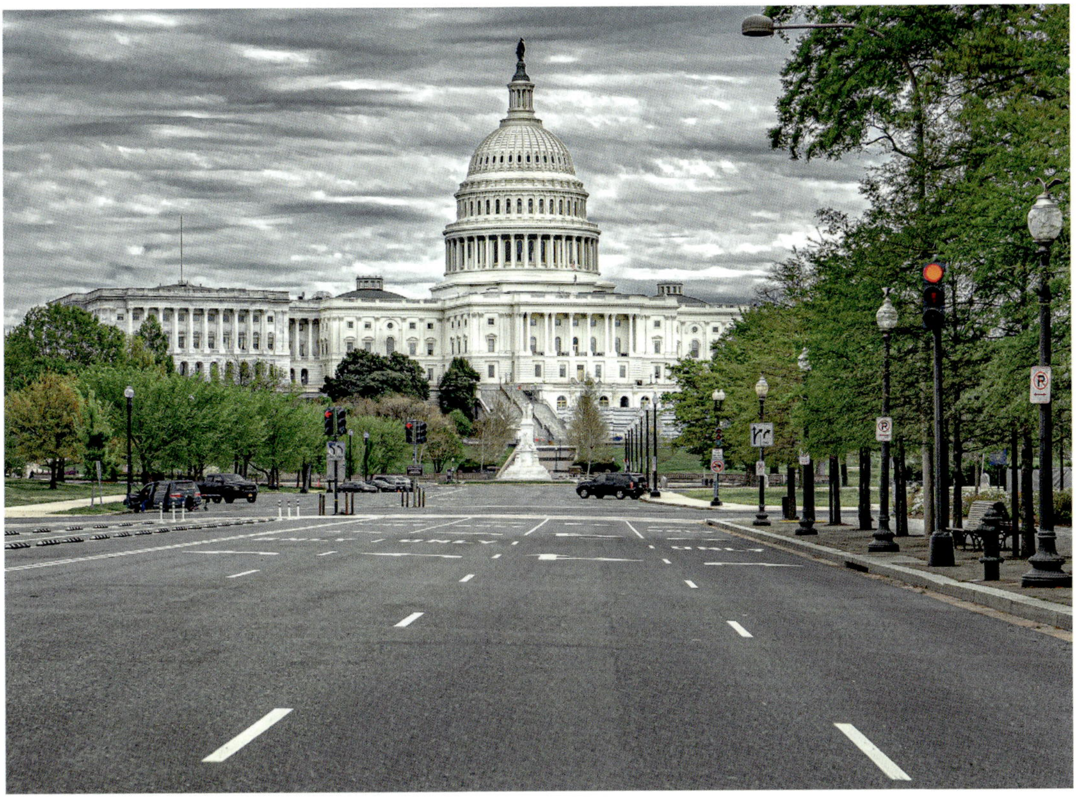

U.S. CAPITOL, PENNSYLVANIA AVENUE: On any normal noontime, this street would be gridlocked with traffic and filled with parked vehicles on the left, and four car-filled rows in front of the Capitol.

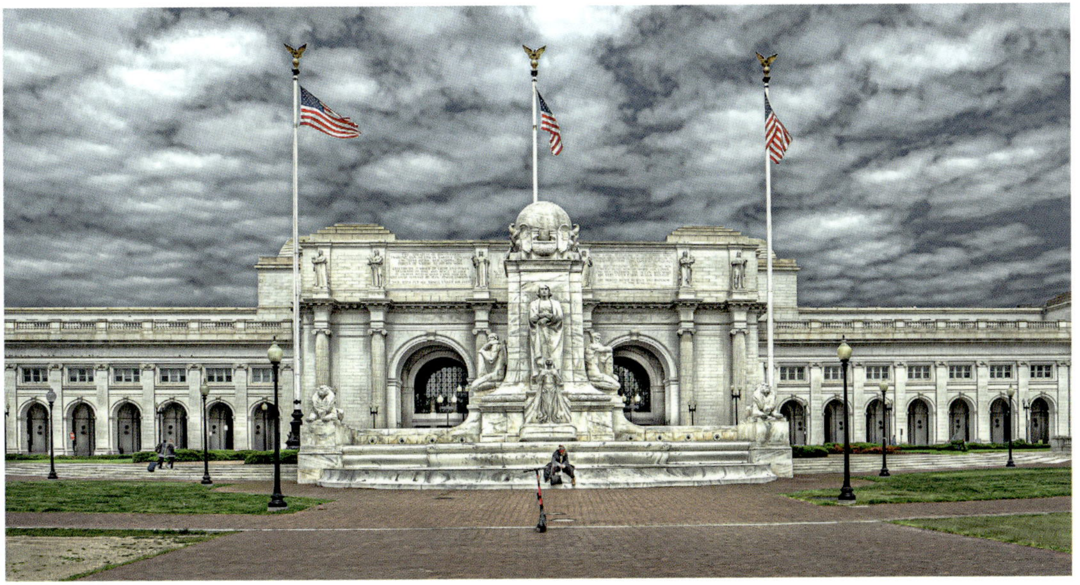

UNION STATION: Our reality. At normal times, this station overflows with travelers, and no matter the hour, a hellish circle of vehicles clogs the entrance area. Now, with COVID, Union Station appears as if its soul departed and will not return.

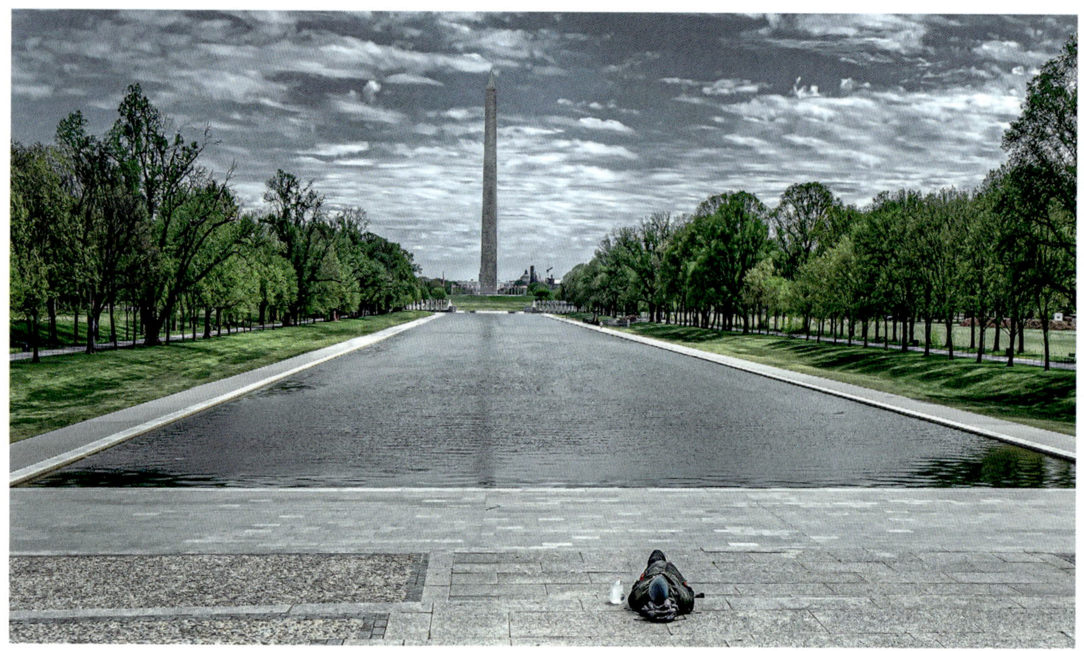

WASHINGTON MONUMENT AND REFLECTING POOL: This view looks like the last man on earth, but this is not a scene from a comedic movie—this is the stark reality in the time of COVID.

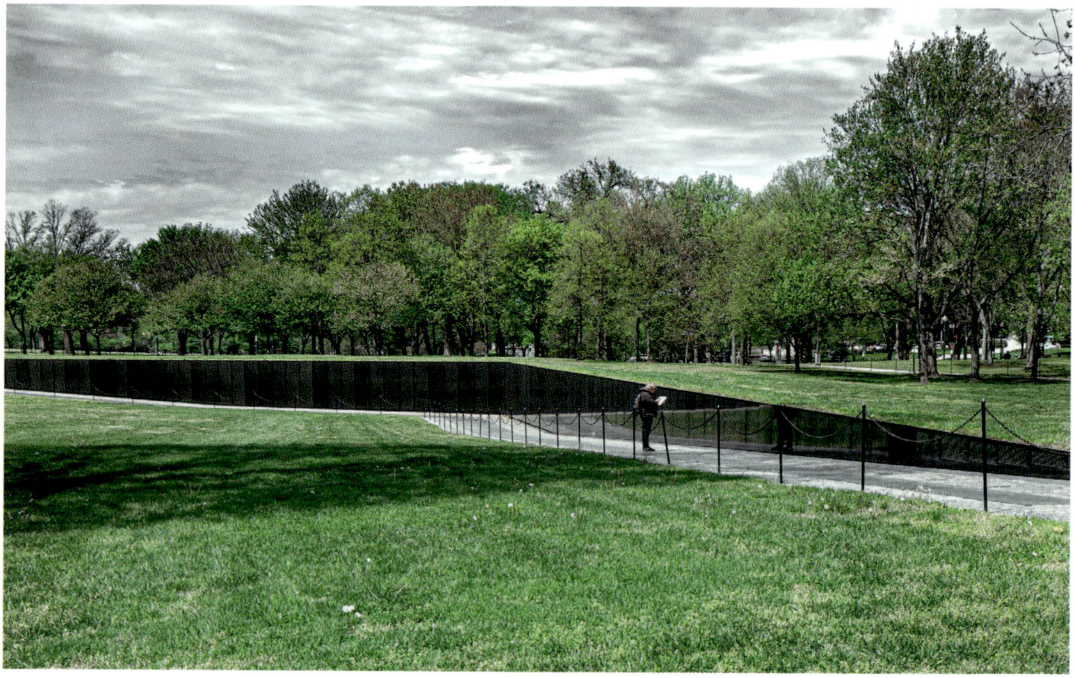

VIETNAM VETERANS MEMORIAL: With no one else in sight, one pays tribute to the fallen at the Vietnam Memorial.

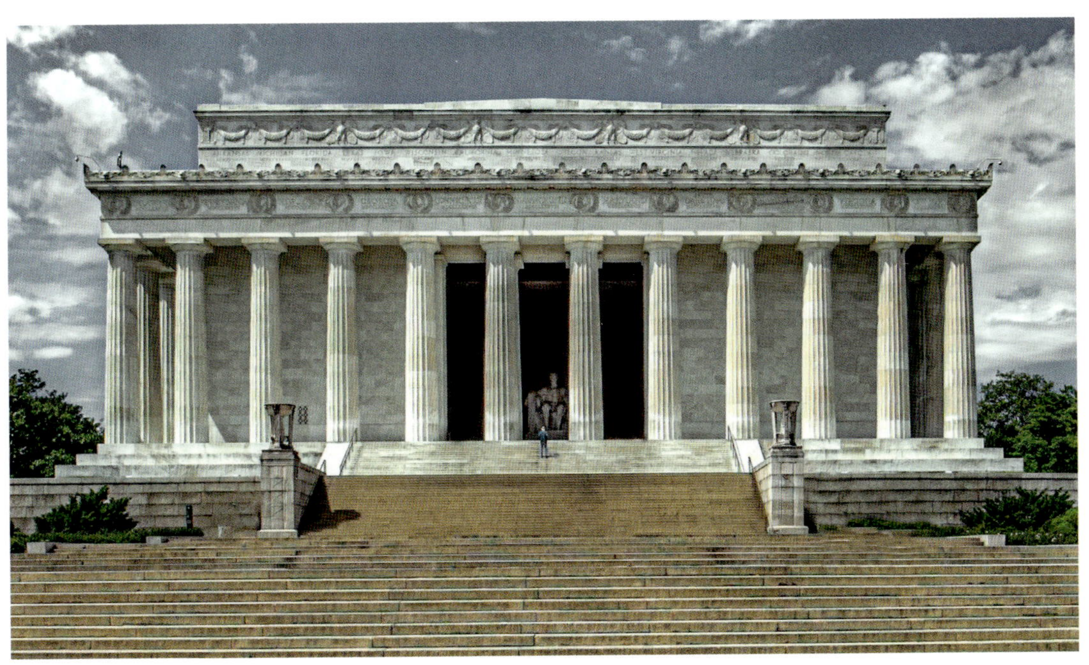

LINCOLN MEMORIAL: It is COVID noon as Lincoln watches over the emptiness of D.C.

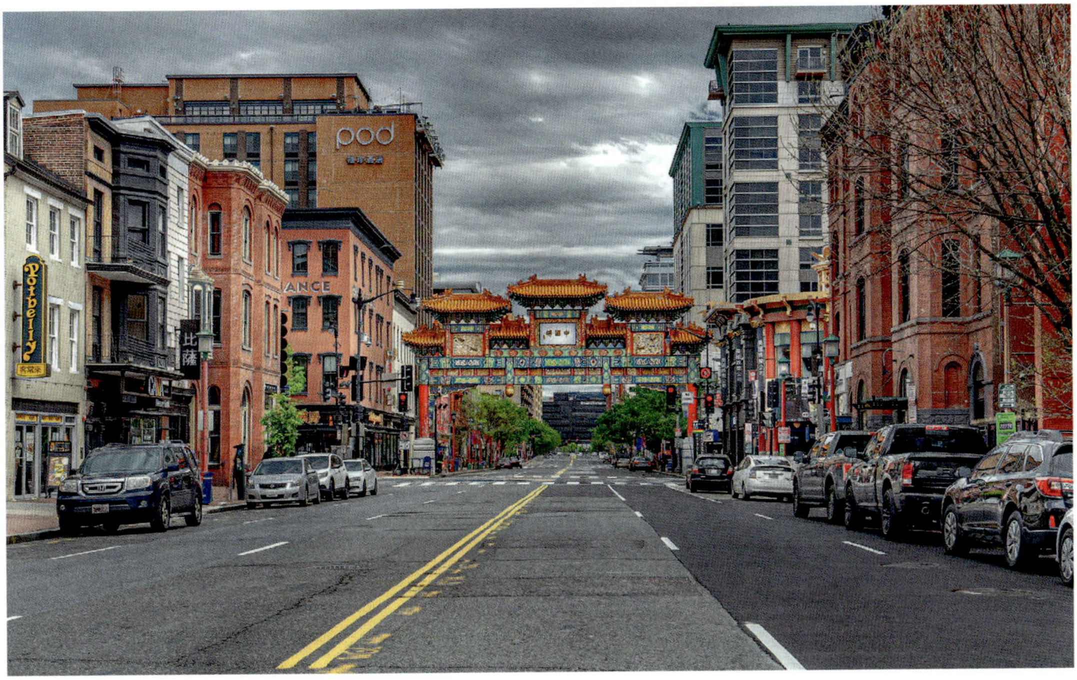

FRIENDSHIP ARCH: This is the silence of noontime in a once busy neighborhood of D.C.

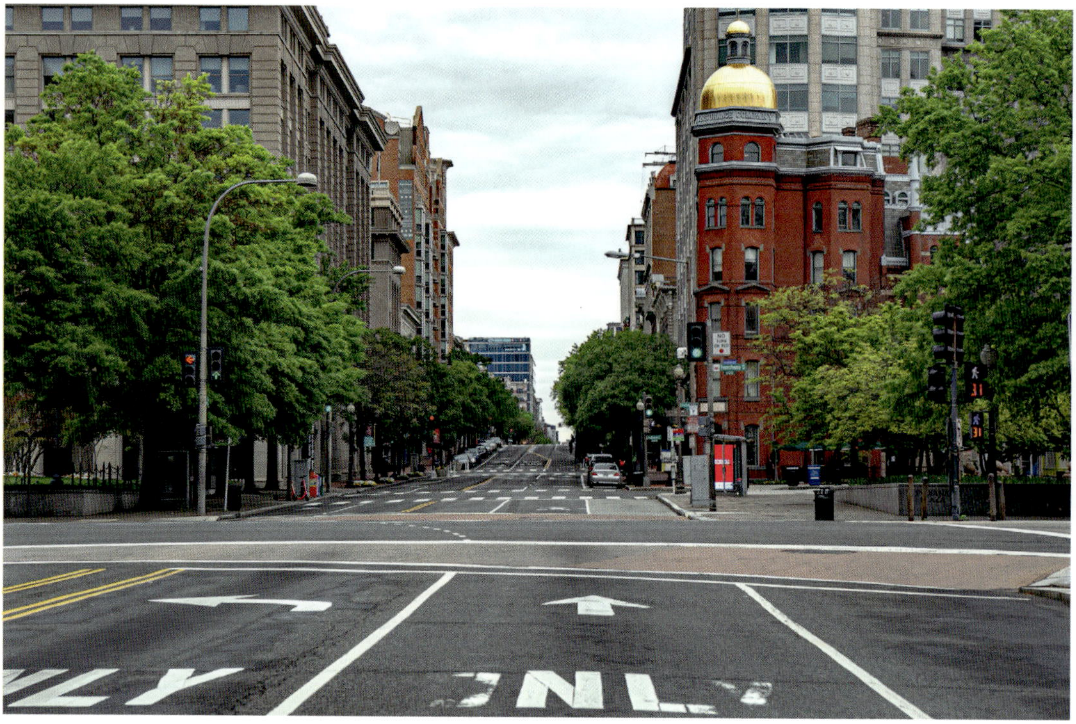

▲ **SILENT STREETS:** The stillness of 4:30 p.m. rush hour at Indiana Plaza-Pennsylvania Avenue and 8th Street—near Penn Quarter.

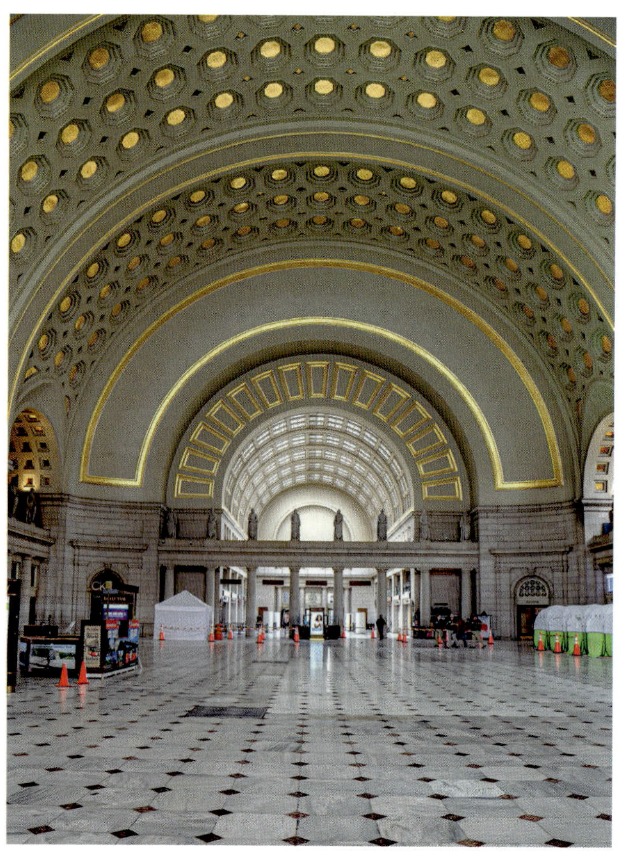

▼ **UNION STATION:** Where are the travelers?

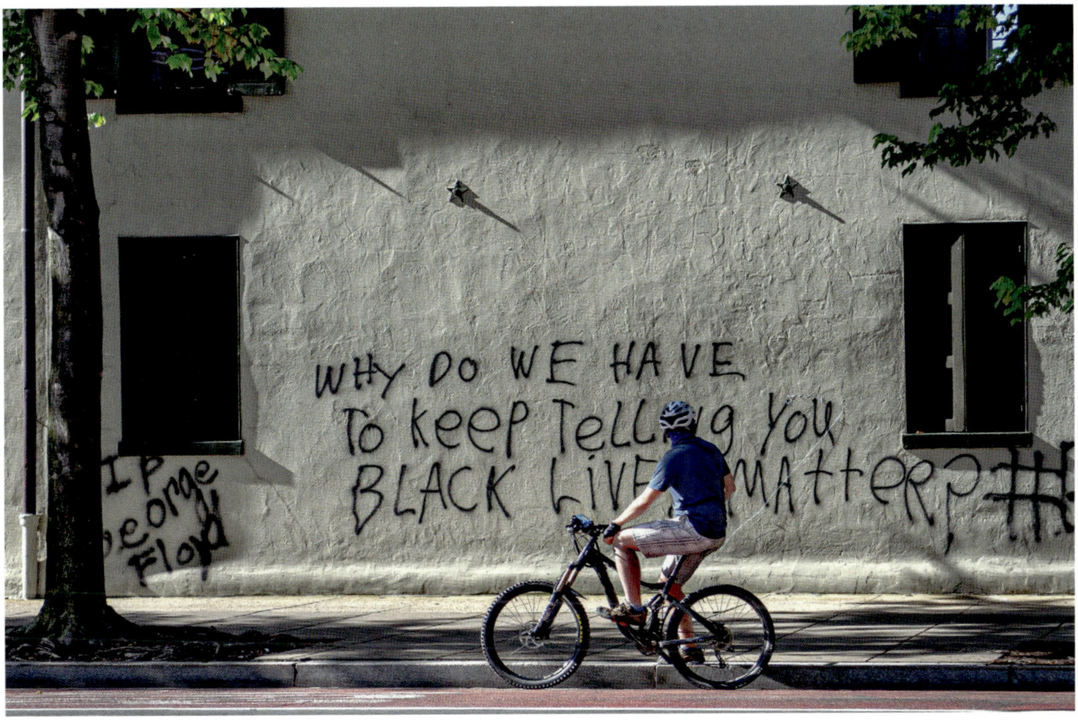

A PAUSE: "The words of the prophets are written on the subway walls and tenement halls." Sounds of Silence, Simon & Garfunkel.

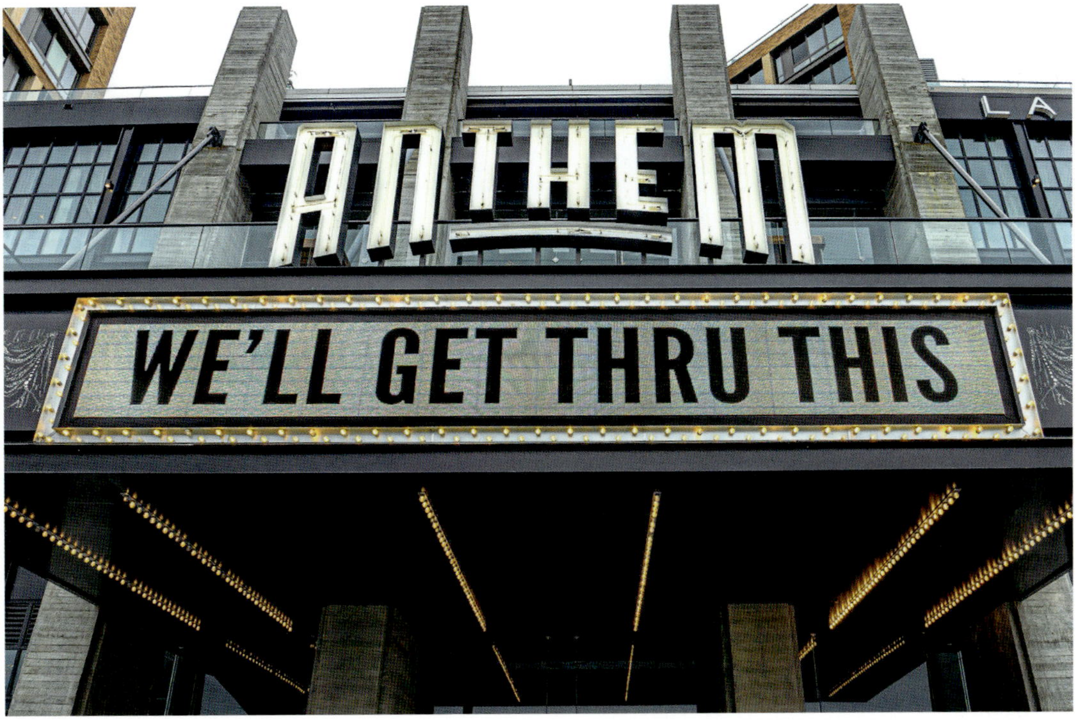

ANTHEM MUSIC VENUE: I hope.

ABOUT THE AUTHOR

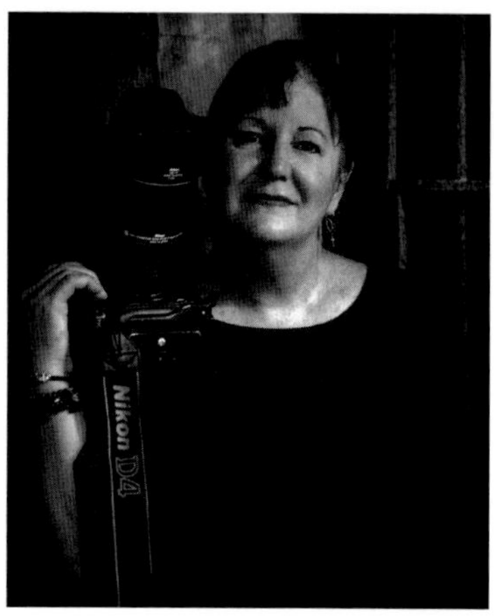

Cindy Vasko was born in Allentown, Pennsylvania, and resides in Arlington, Virginia, near Washington, D.C. For fifteen years, Cindy was the publications manager for a large construction law firm in Northern Virginia, and concurrently, interviewed musicians, wrote articles, and photographed concerts for a music magazine for four years. While Cindy enjoys partaking in all photography genres and is a multi-faceted photographer, she has a passion for abandoned site photography. Cindy is an award-winning photographer with works featured in many gallery exhibitions, including galleries in New York City, Washington, D.C., Philadelphia, Pennsylvania, and Paris, France.

Cindy's Abandoned Union series books include: *Abandoned New York*; *Abandoned Maryland: Lost Legacies*; *Abandoned Western Pennsylvania: Separation from a Proud Heritage*; *Abandoned Catskills: Deserted Playgrounds*; *Abandoned Southern New Jersey: A Bounty of Oddities*; *Abandoned Northern New Jersey: Homage to Lost Dreams*; *Abandoned West Virginia: Crumbling Vignettes*; and coming soon, *Abandoned Eastern Pennsylvania : Remnants of History*; *Abandoned Eastern Ohio: Traces of Fading History*; *Abandoned Northern Virginia: Desolate Beauty*; *Abandoned Southern Virginia: Reckless Surrender*; and, *Abandoned Salton Sea, California: Dystopian Panoramas.*

BIBLIOGRAPHY

Admin. "Home." TheSouthwester.com, 14 Nov. 2012, thesouthwester.com/2012/11/14/from-vacant-to-vibrant-an-old-church-is-transformed/.

"AFRH-W History." *Armed Forces Retirement Home*, 2020, www.afrh.gov/locations/afrh-w-history.

AFRH, "Inspiring Independence, AFRH Performance and Accountability Report," *AFRH,* 2011.

"Architecture of an Asylum: St. Elizabeth's 1852-2017 at the National Building Museum." *National Building Museum*, 25 Mar. 2020, www.nbm.org/exhibition/architecture-asylum-st-elizabeths-1852-2017/.

Bailey, Jeremy. "Deciphering DC: Capitol Stones." *A DC Journey*, 3 Jan. 2018, adcjourney.com/2017/04/13/deciphering-dc-capitol-stones/.

Beachbums1. "Washington DC: Goats and Graves." *Displaced Beachbums*, 13 Aug. 2015, beachbums1.com/2015/08/12/washington-dc-goats-and-graves/.

"A Brief History of Congressional Cemetery." *Historic Congressional Cemetery*, 14 Aug. 2019, congressionalcemetery.org/history/.

BYT at Large. "Hidden in Plain Sight: Wall of Fame." *BrightYoungThings.com*, 13 Oct. 2014, brightestyoungthings.com/articles/hidden-in-plain-sight-wall-of-fame.

Carter, Elliot. "Ruins of the McMillan Sand Filtration Site." *Atlas Obscura*, 16 June 2017, www.atlasobscura.com/places/ruins-of-the-mcmillan-sand-filtration-site.

Carter, Elliot. "The Asylum Where the U.S. Tested Marijuana As a 'Truth Serum' on Nazi Prisoners." *Atlas Obscura*, 18 Oct. 2017, www.atlasobscura.com/places/st-elizabeths.

Carter, Elliot. "The Psychedelic Church in Southwest D.C." *Atlas Obscura*, 10 July 2017, www.atlasobscura.com/places/blind-whino.

davidplotz1. "The Capitol Stones." *Atlas Obscura*, 2 May 2016, www.atlasobscura.com/places/the-capitol-stones-washington-dc.

Einberger, Scott. "History of Carter Barron Amphitheatre." *Rock Creek Conservancy*, 2020, rockcreekconservancy.org/what-we-do/rcc-restoration/restoration-projects/592-the-history-of-carter-barron-amphitheatre.

Fallen, Anne-Catherine, et al. *A Botanic Garden for the Nation: The United States Botanic Garden*. United States Botanic Garden, 2007.

Fenston, Jacob. "All Quacked Out: WWII-Era Duck Boats Have Seemingly Taken Their Last Ride In D.C." *DCist*, 6 Nov. 2019, dcist.com/story/19/11/06/duck-boats-ferried-supplies-on-d-day-tourists-on-the-national-mall-now-theyre-retiring/.

"Franklin School." *Planet Word*, www.planetwordmuseum.org/project-information#about-franklin-school.

Giambrone, Andrew. "Developer Resumes Work on Franklin School Project After Agreeing to Reinstall Historic Fabric." *Curbed DC*, 16 Jan. 2019, dc.curbed.com/2019/1/16/18184257/dc-franklin-school-redevelopment-historic-interiors-agreement.

Haugh , Christopher. "The Silence That Whistles Through the Tombstones." *Narratively*, 22 June 2019, narratively.com/the-silence-that-whistles-through-the-tombstones/.

"The History of McMillan Park & Sand Filtration Plant." *Save McMillan Park*, 2020, savemcmillan.org/history/.

Jacobson, Dorothy. "District of Columbia United Clay Products Company: New York Avenue Brickyard." *Historic American Engineering Record*, U.S. Department of Agriculture, 1983, https://cdn.loc.gov/master/pnp/habshaer/dc/dc0300/dc0346/data/dc0346data.pdf.

Kelly, John. "Perspective I For Two Summers, Carter Barron Amphitheatre Hosted a 'Symphonic Drama'." *The Washington Post*, 21 Sept. 2019, www.washingtonpost.com/local/for-two-summers-carter-barron-amphitheatre-hosted-a-symphonic-drama/2019/09/21/6c7309b0-db0e-11e9-a688-303693fb4b0b_story.html.

Kelly, John. "What Are Those Odd and Distinctive Brick Buildings Near the National Arboretum?" *The Washington Post*, 15 Nov. 2014, www.washingtonpost.com/local/what-are-those-odd-and-distinctive-brick-buildings-near-the-national-arboretum/2014/11/15/d483a090-6922-11e4-b053-65cea7903f2e_story.html.

Kurzius, Rachel. "McMillan, D.C.'s Most Cursed Development Project, Explained." *DCist*, 31 Jan. 2020, dcist.com/story/20/01/27/mcmillan-d-c-s-most-cursed-development-project-explained/.

Lefrak, Mikaela. "Here's What D.C.'s New 'Planet Word' Museum in The Franklin School Will Look Like." *WAMU*, WAMU 88.5 - American University Radio, 5 June 2018, wamu.org/story/18/06/05/heres-d-c-s-new-planet-word-museum-franklin-school-will-look-like/.

Mosley.Brian. "A Look at Saint Elizabeth's West Campus." *We Love DC*, 21 May 2011, www.welovedc.com/2011/06/03/a-look-at-saint-elizabeths-west-campus/.

Nikki. "Capitol Drift: The National Arboretum." *City to Trail*, 12 Dec. 2016, citytotrail.me/2016/12/11/national-arboretum/.

Oxford Academic. "The Exceptionalism of St. Elizabeth's Hospital in Washington, DC." *Medium*, History Uncut, 21 Aug. 2019, medium.com/history-uncut/the-exceptionalism-of-st-elizabeths-hospital-in-washington-dc-ff641619221b.

Paul, Shilpi. "One on One: Making Murals To Transform a City" *UrbanTurf*, 18 Mar. 2013, dc.urbanturf.com/articles/blog/one_on_one_making_murals_to_transform_a_city/6798.

Pierov, Borys. "2017–01–18 / Dupont Underground-A Guided Tour." *Medium*, Ashald Blog, 23 Mar. 2017, medium.com/ashald/2017-01-18-dupont-underground-a-guided-tour-48f0f6ac478b.

Relocation of Architect's Tree Nursery: Hearings and Markups before the Subcommittee on Fiscal Affairs and Health and the Committee on the District of Columbia, House of Representatives, Ninety-Eighth Congress, First and Second Session, on H.R. 4153 and Substitute H.R. 5565, October 25, 1983, March 15, and May 3, 1984. U.S. G.P.O., 1984.

Replace or Modernize? The Future of District of Columbia's Endangered Old and Historic Public Schools. 21st Century School Fund , May 2001, www.21csf.org/csf-home/publications/ReplaceorModernize.pdf.

Richards, Daniel. "The Curious Rise of Historic Trolley Tours." *Atlas Obscura*, 19 Sept. 2017, www.atlasobscura.com/articles/history-trolley-tours.

Sauber, Jenna. *From Classrooms to Language Museum: D.C.'s Historic Franklin School Has New Purpose: National Trust for Historic Preservation*. 15 Sept. 2017, savingplaces.org/stories/from-classrooms-to-a-language-museum-dcs-historic-franklin-school-has-a-new-purpose#.XwxwTS05RUN.

Schweitzer, Ally. *The Sorrow and The Beauty: D.C.'s St. Elizabeth's*. WAMU 88.5 - American University Radio, 30 Mar. 2017, wamu.org/story/17/03/29/sorrow-beauty-d-c-s-st-elizabeths/.

Separate and Unequal: The State of the District of Columbia Public Schools Fifty Years after Brown and Bolling. A Parents United for the D.C. Public Schools Civic Leader Advisory Committee Report, Mar. 2005, www.washlaw.org/pdf/Separate_and_Unequal_Report.pdf.

Shuler, Madison. *"The Art of Vandalism": A Built Environment Analysis of Edgewood Washington, D.C.* Madison Shuler, 2020, edspace.american.edu/ms4241a/the-art-of-vandalism/.

Silvestri , Mike. "Thurgood Marshall's Abandoned, Run-Down Elementary School to Undergo Historic Preservation." *Washington Examiner*, 16 Mar. 2012, www.washingtonexaminer.com/thurgood-marshall-s-abandoned-run-down-elementary-school-to-undergo-historic-preservation.

"Soldier's Home, Main Building (Sherman Building)." *DC Historic Sites*, 2020, historicsites.dcpreservation.org/items/show/562.

Svrluga, Susan. "Smithsonian Experts Restore Historic Vault, Find Unexpected Connection to Shriver Family." *The Washington Post*, 11 June 2014, www.washingtonpost.com/local/smithsonian-restores-historic-vault-with-shriver-family-ancestors/2014/06/11/e94c0408-f1a0-11e3-9ebc-2ee6f81ed217_story.html.

United States, Congress, National Park Service. *National Register of Historic Places Inventory - Nomination Form for Federal Properties – United Brick Corporation*, ser. PH0503126, 1977. https://npgallery.nps.gov/GetAsset/4a04fc19-5c64-4232-9355-24b790b8296c

WhiskeyBristles. "Long-Abandoned Trolley Tunnels Near the White House." *Atlas Obscura*, 6 Mar. 2017, www.atlasobscura.com/places/dupont-underground.

WhiskeyBristles1. "Ruins of the Forgotten Brickyard That Helped Build the Nation's Capital." *Atlas Obscura*, 9 Feb. 2017, www.atlasobscura.com/places/united-brick-corporation-ruins.